Leaders without Titles

Stephen J. Sampson, Ph.D.

HRD Press, Inc. • Amherst • Massachusetts

Published by: HRD Press, Inc.
                  22 Amherst Road
                  Amherst, MA 01002
                  800-822-2801 (U.S. and Canada)
                  413-253-3488
                  413-253-3490 (fax)
                  www.hrdpress.com

ISBN 978-1-59996-250-4

Production services by Jean Miller
Cover design by Eileen Klockars
Editorial work by Sally M. Farnham

Dr. Sampson has offered an understanding into the dynamics of leadership and the thinking that creates leaders, both men and women, in a structured, easily understood pattern that reads like a novel, builds to a climax and, most importantly, delivers like a text without the rote that so easily stumbles the reader. Read it two times. It's worth even more the second time around.

O'Neill Williams, Radio and Television Personality, "O'Neill Outdoors"

In any organizational environment there are individuals to whom others look for guidance, direction, and leadership. Very often those persons are not the highest ranking members of the organization. Why? Dr. Sampson provides an insightful analysis of the complex array of factors that cause some persons to become leaders while others can only manage. This is a must read to understand these critical dynamics.

Gary Deland, Executive Director, Utah Sheriff's Association

Leaders without Titles is a must read for anyone in leadership or aspiring to become a leader. The six attributes identified to complete a leader make the reader aware of the importance of recognizing informal authority in individuals, especially in the workplace. All leaders, managers and supervisors should read this book; it can be used as a "must read" for the management team to develop their social intelligence skills to better manage the informal leaders in the organization. It is an easy read with examples of real-life stories, complete with a self-administered assessment at the end of each chapter.

Dr. Sampson is an expert on developing social intelligence skills for leadership, and can adapt to any audience using practical applications to bring out the leader within.

Dr. Winnifred McPherson, Retired Major, Broward County Sheriff's Department

There is a powerful tendency to blindly idolize leaders with psychopathic tendencies who can take over a government or company and literally "cut throats" without a conscience. On a larger scale, these are often charismatic leaders who can set in motion the slaughter of millions, as in the case of Adolph Hitler.

In contrast to these powerful but dangerous leaders, Steve Sampson focuses on the prerequisite qualities that can be developed and honed by individuals into effective leadership with a moral compass. While DNA certainly can be an innate part of one's leadership ability, the skill sets needed to become an effective leader are definable "learned" behavior. In *Leaders without Titles*, Dr. Sampson provides a blueprint for the development of what he believes to be the six essential dimensions of leadership. Similar to all of his work, the material is presented in a practical, straightforward approach that not only allows the reader to understand the theoretical underpinnings of each dimension, but also practice the concepts involved. In order to gauge proficiency as the skills are being developed, a method for testing is provided.

Because we believe so strongly in Dr. Sampson's approach to teaching interpersonal communication skills and leadership dimensions, his body of work is being incorporated as a vital part of the curriculum available to all of the undergraduate and graduate degree programs located in the College of Justice and Safety.

Dr. Allen Ault, Dean, College of Justice & Safety, Eastern Kentucky University

When attempting to teach new leaders how to influence and lead others, I often ask them to think about the best and worst leaders they have ever had. I then ask them to list the behaviors, characteristics or traits that made them the best or worse. Without fail, these fledgling leaders list behaviors or characteristics that describe what *kind of person* the leader was: could they trust the person; how did the person interact with and treat other people; was the person honest and honorable. I believe that Dr. Sampson has captured the essence of what makes a person a good and effective leader, whether or not that person has any formal authority. He has identified, and clearly examines and explains six personal attributes which naturally garner the trust and confidence of others. Imagine what a great and powerful leader one could be if he or she not only had the formal authority, but also demonstrated the attributes identified by Dr. Sampson! He has shown us a pathway to successful leadership, whether we have the title or not!

William M. Allen, President, Bill Allen and Associate, Inc.

In *Leaders without Titles*, Steve Sampson makes the brilliant case that leadership is no longer a function of position, fear, money or authority alone, but rather results from being socially authentic. His six powerful attributes of influence should inform the honest heart and realign leadership practices across disciplines including those of academia, government, business and even the military. An enlightening and easy to read book that will change the way leaders see themselves and their subordinates.

An excellent leadership text and gift! Dr. Steve Sampson demonstrates once again that he is the ultimate expert in leading people by being personable. His leaders don't cajole, bribe or demand—they influence. This book should be required reading in every government and military leadership training program and all university business programs. The result could be an entire generation of new leaders uniquely poised to change the way America's workforce confronts tomorrow's most challenging problems.

Dr. Russell Baker, Special Operations Intelligence Psychologist

It has become painfully commonplace for notable authors to quote lists of action items necessary to "be a good leader." In fact, we all know in our hearts that the most significant steps anyone manages to achieve in their leadership journey really involves deep personal reflection and self-actualization. Dr. Sampson has done a masterful job of capturing the most critical attributes required for an individual's personal evolutionary process to be meaningful and effective. Clearly, without the desire to improve as individuals, studying the philosophy of leadership is marginally productive at best. The adage of leading one's self before others has withstood the test of time and that makes *Leaders without Titles* an excellent resource for all of us who are constantly striving to improve regardless of positional authority.

David N. Boggs, Deputy Chief of Police, Lexington Division of Police

Table of Contents

Preface

What does it mean to lead? Are there natural born leaders? Can leadership be taught? These questions have consumed this writer for years since his first formal leadership role at 23 years old.

Since words are often the place to start when defining a concept such as leading, the following are some definitions from the *Oxford American Dictionary* of the words *lead* and *leader:*

> **lead:** "Cause to go with by guiding or showing the way; direct the actions or opinions of others; guide others by persuasion, example, or argument; provide access to; bring to certain destination; pass or go through; have first place in a race/competition; be in charge; direct by example."

> **leader:** "A person or thing that leads; a person followed by others; the head, chief, commander, director, principal of something; the pace setter, trend setter, front runner, innovator, pioneer, pathfinder, ground breaker, originator of something."

In general, one could say that the words *lead* and *leader* are associated with terms and phrases like *power, control, regulate, preside over, prompt, move, conduct, guide, oversee, persuade, induce rule, govern,* etc. Given this information and terminology, it is apparent that leaders lead others to some goal (large or small) that the others might not have achieved unless the leader forced, modeled, motivated, or guided them into doing so.

Usually leaders do this through formal authority, which is determined by designated title or rank given to these leaders. This formal authority enables leaders to lead not through their actual abilities but by virtue of their formal titles.

There are other factors, both innate and learned, that enable leaders to lead without formal authority. Knowing what these are is critical in understanding how to be a leader. Individuals can possess abilities that make people want to follow their lead or direction. This is the focus of this book.

Chapter 1

Introduction

The goal of this book is two-fold. The first is to challenge the way we determine who our leaders should be. Should leaders be chosen based on the formal education they achieve? Should they be determined by public perception, i.e., elections? Should they be determined and allowed to lead based on formally acquired leadership, rank, or title? Should they be chosen based on their socio-economic privilege and status?

The above factors should be considered as relevant in the right to lead. They may be necessary; however, they may not be sufficient.

The second and primary focus is to examine what other factors influence the ability to lead beyond the factors named above. Are there factors besides these that should determine who should lead? Are they synonymous with the idea of a "natural leader"? Are there traits in persons that empower them over others without formal authority?

A mentor of mine once said to me that "to influence without authority was the key to leadership." The idea was that force/formal authority was not the primary way to lead; in fact, it should be the last resort when leading. This statement had a tremendous effect on me when I heard it over 30 years ago because up until that point I believed that formal authority was the key to leading—that a person's formal rank as well as the rules and regulations determine leadership outcomes.

Since that time, my quest has been to look for leadership in other places other than formal authority. Once I found what these leading-without-authority factors could be, this book came into being.

I therefore entitled this book *Leaders without Titles*. I decided to use this title after struggling with how to articulate what influencing others without authority is. Thanks to my colleague Norman Spain, a professor at Eastern Kentucky University College of Justice and Safety, I developed this title, and I thank him.

There are people who are not in the formal position of authority who are able to convince or coerce people to do things. They are often more powerful than those given the formal authority over others. In observing these informal leaders, I realized that if formal leaders had these informal leader attributes, their ability to motivate others to action could be even greater.

We know that individuals are drawn to people who may not have formal authority over them. These people are often described as charismatic. They have human attributes that attract others to them and therefore have influence over others. These informal power attributes can be divided into six (6) categories: physicality, intellectuality, sociability, emotionality, personability, and morality. Let's discuss each briefly. The book will later devote a chapter to each.

Physicality

The first and most common power attribute would be a person's physicality. A person who is seen by others as physically powerful, attractive, or healthy can have significant influence over others.

The physicality attribute is probably best exemplified by our attraction to athletes in our society. The physical power and skills they display draw people to them. Athletes are typically idolized by adoring fans. This adoration gives them significant power and influence over others. Because of their influence over the minds and actions of others, they are often paid to endorse products through advertising.

For this reason, you rarely see a leading man or woman in a movie that would be described as unattractive physically. These men and women are usually taller than the average person and well-defined in body proportion with attractive faces and eyes. It is interesting then that they are classified as "leading" men and women. Like athletes, due to their physical attractiveness and the celebrity status that goes with it, these leading actors and actresses can easily influence the minds and actions of others.

Intellectuality

The second power attribute to informal leadership is intellectual attraction. Intellectual attraction is the ability to use one's thinking as a motivator of others. The term *beautiful mind* often describes this attribute.

A beautiful mind can be demonstrated by one's ability to think outside the norm of thinking, to conceptualize or develop ideas and strategies to solve problems, and to utilize logical processing of information quality before acting on it. It is not necessarily a measure of someone's performance on an IQ test.

People are drawn to intellectually attractive persons because they possess knowledge that others often need to understand life and their existence. In other words, they possess knowledge critical to living. Doctors and teachers are often seen in this way, but Albert Einstein represents the intellectuality leadership more than anyone. Walter Issacson, author of a biography on Einstein, said the following:

> Einstein was more creative than others at the time partly because he was more rebellious. Just because Newton said that time marches along, second by second, independent of our observations, that didn't mean Einstein accepted that as gospel. He said, "How do we know that?" Even when he was just a patent examiner in 1905, he was challenging the basic assumptions of modern physics— challenging the notion that time and space are absolute, challenging the notion that light is a wave as opposed to being both a wave and a particle. These are great leaps of the imagination.

> His fingerprints are all over today's technologies. Whether you look at photoelectric cells or lasers or nuclear power or space travel or GPS systems or semiconductors, all of these trace back to his theories. The two most important theories of the 20th century— relativity and quantum theory—were both born out of Einstein's head when he was a patent clerk, and almost all of the technologies that define our century are touched by this.... (Isaacson, 2007).

Though Einstein was known to be a poor student in his formal education, and he was only a patent clerk when his theories became known, he is still the most recognized and cited intellectual in science today.

Sociability

A third power attribute that informal leaders have is sociability. Sociability is defined as fitted for or liking the society of others. These people are ready and willing to engage others without anxiety or fear. They exhibit nonverbal communication and verbal communication skills that draw others to them. They rarely act at a loss for words, and their nonverbal behaviors display confidence when engaging with others. Those without sociability are usually described as introverted, shy, and difficult to talk to.

Examples of social leaders' characteristics are found in politicians and religious leaders. In his book, *Age of Turbulence*, Allen Greenspan describes former President Bill Clinton as having the sociability attribute. Initially Greenspan was reluctant to work for the Democratic Clinton since Greenspan was initially appointed by a Republican president and considered himself a Republican. Greenspan stated that after his initial, several-hours-long meeting with Clinton, he was willing to stay on as Chair of the Federal Reserve Bank. He described Clinton as having an incredible ability to give undivided attention to another and to remember everything that was said (Greenspan, 2007). Clinton clearly had the sociability attribute as one of his strengths, but his lacking of some others eventually led to his downfall.

Emotionality

A fourth power attribute that informal leaders possess is emotionality. Emotionality is the ability to utilize emotions to move others. Many cultures teach that displaying emotions should be controlled, while others do not. This is probably due to the fact that emotions are powerful in their influence over ourselves and others. In fact, science has shown that emotions can be contagious. People who are emotional can draw out both positive and negative emotions in others. Angry leaders can motivate people to attack or challenge someone/something. Fearful leaders can motivate people to flee when encountering something or someone. Happy leaders can draw people toward them/others in a positive way.

Emotions can also bias our thinking. We often oppose thoughts or facts that do not support our emotions and conversely welcome those who do.

Persons who can emotionalize can be powerful because they use their emotions to not only affect others' emotions but also to influence the subsequent actions and thoughts of others.

Of course inappropriate emotionalizing—quickness to anger, fear, and sadness—can inhibit one's ability to lead. Examples of emotional leaders are typically sports coaches, motivational speakers, and spiritual leaders. Vince Lombardi, the famous coach of the Green Bay Packers, was known for his emotionality in motivating players to compete and win. During his career, his teams won five national football championships. The following quote illustrates his emotionality:

> I don't say these things because I believe in the "brute" nature of man or that men must be brutalized to be combative. I believe in God, and I believe in human decency. But I firmly believe that any man's finest hour—his greatest fulfillment to all he holds dear—is that moment when he has to **work his heart** out in a good cause and **he's exhausted** on the field of battle—victorious.

Vince Lomdardi's use of the phrase *work his heart* shows his belief that emotion is critical to motivating and succeeding.

Personability

The fifth power attribute, personability, is probably the most difficult to achieve because it requires being hard on oneself. John Wooden, who was voted Coach of the Century in 2009 at the age of 99, was known for his selfless, humble, nondeceptive approach to leadership and life. During his 27-year career as head coach of the UCLA Bruins, he never had a losing season and won ten NCAA basketball championships.

Wooden, who grew up poor on a farm in Indiana, came to be a college basketball coach in a rather roundabout way. As a matter of fact, Wooden intended to become a civil engineer when he entered Purdue University, but instead majored in English and played basketball. Despite being offered a spot on the Boston Celtics, he took a position teaching English so that he could marry his high school sweetheart. Wooden coached high school basketball and ultimately coached college ball at Indiana State Teachers College—this led to him being offered a position as head coach at UCLA in 1948.

For all of Wooden's conventional successes, he did not define success or measure it in terms of scores or winning percentages. According to Wooden, success is "peace of mind attained only through self-satisfaction in knowing you made the effort to become the best of which you're capable" ("John Wooden Biography—Academy of Achievement," 2010). People who are personable, like Wooden, are described as approachable, unselfish, real, and unassuming. They are probably this way because they accept responsibility when things go wrong around them, rather than blame others or circumstances.

Sandra Day O'Connor, a recently retired Supreme Court Justice, exemplifies the personability in leadership based on people's perception of her in the following anecdote:

> A colleague of mine was sitting in the coach section of a flight from the East coast to the West coast. She noticed a lady sitting next to her by the window. She said she kept glancing over at her thinking that it was Justice Sandra Day O'Connor. She felt her perception must be wrong because she couldn't imagine someone of her stature riding in the coach section of an airplane.
>
> Finally she stated she couldn't contain her need to ask her if she was in fact Justice Sandra Day O'Connor. When she did, the passenger confirmed that she was Justice Sandra Day O'Connor.
>
> My colleague stated that from that point on that Ms. O'Connor and she talked the whole flight. She stated that Justice O'Connor was transparent, with no airs and very open about her life. My colleague said she was in awe of how comfortable Justice O'Connor made her feel while riding in coach on a trans-continental flight.

Though considerable importance was placed on Justice O'Connor being the first woman appointed to the Supreme Court *and* her influence on the Court (she was often the deciding "swing" vote in many decisions), her early career in law was fairly unremarkable. In fact, when she first graduated from Stanford Law School in 1950, she was unsuccessful in securing a position for herself in firms in San Francisco and Los Angeles *because* she was a woman.

On her appointment to the Supreme Court, Day O'Connor said in 2000, "My concern was whether I could do the job of a justice well enough to convince the nation that my appointment was the right one."

O'Connor's unpretentious assessment of her abilities as a jurist illustrate the degree to which she can be seen as a genuine individual, despite the prestige and status her position afforded her.

It is possible that individuals can have attributes in all of the above in varying degrees, but it would be rare to find an individual who possesses high functioning in the first five attributes discussed here. Achievement of such would be difficult to attain without dedicated development in each over a lifetime.

Heredity can also play a significant role in having the above attributes because our DNA can be critical in determining our destiny in terms of physicality, sociability, emotionality, intellectuality, and personability.

Despite DNA's power, it is possible that dedicated focus can override one's genetic predispositions. Conversely, people with natural gifts (heredity) in any of the above attributes often waste or do not apply them.

Moral Ability

The sixth dimension critical to proper application of the above five informal leadership abilities is moral ability. Moral ability is the attribute of knowing and applying the principle of fairness and goodness versus evil and unfairness in how one conducts his or her life.

The moral attribute is the most difficult to define because it is influenced by so many variables, including the five abilities mentioned above. The most significant variable is probably a spiritual one. Moral development has historically been aligned with spirituality or religion. Concepts such as sin, karma, heaven, and hell have been connected to morality.

The variety of religions in the world and varying interpretations of moral thought and actions often convolute its definitions and applications. Historically and presently, many acts of immorality such as war have been directly related to or justified by religious beliefs and institutions. This is why our forefathers sought to separate church from state as a governing principle in democracy as well as providing religious freedom to the American citizenry.

Conversely, an argument for religion's influence on moral actions and thinking in a positive way can also be documented historically. The argument that it is not the religious principles that are immoral but the human interpretation of and application utilizing religious doctrine is what needs to be addressed. Many individuals have used religion in ways that advocated immoral behaviors. Let's look at the example of Jim Jones below.

> Jim Jones was the founder of the Peoples Temple. The Peoples Temple was initially structured as an interracial mission for the sick, homeless, and jobless. It began in the Indianapolis, Indiana, area in the 1950s and preached a gospel of social equality, love, and freedom.

> In the 1970s, an exposé in *New West* magazine raised suspicions about illegal activities within the Peoples Temple. A government investigation raised concerns about Peoples Temple claims for cures for cancer, heart disease, and arthritis. As a result, Jones moved his church to 4,000 acres of leased land to what he called Jonestown, Guyana.

> Jones preached a concept of "Translation" in which his followers would all die together and move to another planet. Mass suicides were simulated utilizing a poisoned drink. Jones was reported to have been abusing prescription drugs. Relatives of Peoples Temple members and others who left the Peoples Temple claimed that human rights abuses were being perpetrated at the Peoples Temple; they also claimed it was being run like a concentration camp.

When Leo Ryan, a Congressman, visited Jones in 1978 for an investigation, heavily armed security guards of the Peoples Temple shot at him and his party as they attempted to leave with 16 Temple members wanting to flee the camp.

Following this event, the remaining members, approximately 638 adults and 276 children, committed mass suicide along with Jones. The suicide involved the drinking of grape juice loaded with cyanide, sedatives, valium, penegram, and chloral hydrate. A subsequent investigation revealed that hundreds may have been murdered. ("WGBH American Experience. Jonestown: The Life and Death of Peoples Temple. Introduction," n.d.)

Clearly, Jones's power and influence over his followers was such that it prevented them from seeing right from wrong. While Jones's initial intentions may have been to serve a higher power and help the meek and powerless, those intentions were ultimately metamorphosed into something wicked.

In recent years, there has been a movement to examine morality outside the spiritual realm. It attempts to apply scientific method explanations to the study of morality. It suggests that since scientific method can be applied to our physicality, sociability, emotionality, intellectuality, and personability, it should be able to be applied to morality. This poses the question: is morality hardwired into DNA and therefore scientifically explainable?

Francis Collins's book *The Language of God* attempts to do just that. Collins, a world renowned scientist, led the mapping of DNA for the U.S. government and was recently appointed as the Director of the National Institute of Health. Collins believes that DNA could be God's language. For a well-respected scientist to take such a position indicates a movement of trying to bridge science with spirituality.

In this modern era of cosmology, evolution and human genome, is there still a possibility of a richly satisfying harmony between the scientific and spiritual worlds? I answer with a resounding yes (Collins, 2006).

Several other books, including *The Science of Good and Evil* by Michael Shermer, *The Neuroscience of Fair Play* by Donald Pfaff, and *The Spiritual Brain* by Mario Beauregard and Denyse O'Leary, are attempts to look at morality from a scientific perspective as well as a spiritual one. They all present both logical and scientific arguments for morality's scientific basis as well as spiritual. Regardless of the position one takes on morality as science or spirituality or both, moral application of power through moral leadership is critical.

Historically, the use of formal leadership and informal leadership attributes have been and can be destructive when moral attributes are not used in conjunction with them.

A person who has the physical, social, emotional, intellectual, personable, and moral attributes described above would be a powerful person in their own right even if they were not in a leadership role. This power comes from them emulating characteristics that many others want to replicate in themselves. They are models for what some might describe as the complete human being. To lead not only means to be in charge, but to be the model for how people should act within an organization. To ignore moral ability due to its often inappropriate use of religion does not preclude it from being necessary for human function. The story of Enron Corporation reinforces the need for moral leadership.

> The collapse of the Enron Corporation is an example of how leaders who do not model morality can destroy a company and the lives of people who work there.

> Enron began in 1985 when Kenneth Lay put together a merger between the Houston Gas Company and Internorth, Inc. to form a huge energy corporation.

> In 1986 Lay hired Richard Kinder to run Enron. Kinder's management style was described as transparent and accountable, and he had involvement in every level of the organization. Kinder was described as a very even-handed person to whom you'd better not lie. Kinder also fostered a family-like atmosphere where he showed

concern for the personal lives of everyone who worked there, no matter what their position.

Kinder ran Enron as president from 1986 to 1996. The company reported increased earnings from $202 million to $584 million while its revenues went from $5.3 billion to $13.4 billion. Kinder apparently modeled social, emotional, intellectual, personable, and moral leadership.

In 1997, in a surprising move, Lay named Jeffrey Skilling president and COO and Kinder left, having been betrayed by Lay. Skilling subsequently pursued an aggressive investment strategy for Enron wherein the company became the largest wholesaler of natural gas and electricity. To ensure that Enron employed only the best, Skilling implemented a system called the "Performance Review Committee" nicknamed "Rank and Yank," where periodically the bottom performing 10 percent of Enron employees were fired.

Skilling's approach led to a system of behind-the-scenes manipulation and deception within the organization that included Enron engaging in "market to market" accounting so that future profits could be counted in the present. Skilling's leadership eventually brought out the worst in Enron employees, i.e., selfishness, greed, and deception.

In the end, Enron could not maintain its fraudulent accounting practices, and it collapsed, leading to criminal indictments of Lay, Skilling, and other corporate leaders. Skilling, among others, was convicted and sentenced to prison. Lay later died of an apparent heart attack prior to his criminal sentencing. Several thousand employees lost their jobs and Enron investors lost all of their financial future. (Wikipedia, n.d.)

It appears that when Kenneth Lay gave company control to Jeffrey Skilling, he allowed for a leadership model of poor social, emotional, intellectual, personable, and moral principles.

The goal of this book is to describe the physical, social, emotional, intellectual, personable, and moral attributes of complete people and "how" to achieve them. It also will possibly set the standard for how we select leaders before we place them in positions of power. Human beings who strive to be complete people are likely to be complete leaders.

Technologizing Leadership

The second goal of this book is to ask the reader to consider another new concept in leadership development called human technology.

Before discussing human technology, the term *technology* needs to be expanded upon. Technology is the study of (ology) technique (techn). It is basically a study of applying a particular methodology, art, or application; it is not theoretical or conceptual. Applications are as important as theories because they can ultimately alter our realities.

P.W. Bridgman, a Nobel Prize-winning physicist, stated, "The true meaning of a term is to be found by observing what a human does with it not by what he or she says about it." Bridgman made enormous contributions to science by demonstrating that the meaning of a scientific term lies in its operations, or "actions"—the things it does. The actions or technologies establish the scientific validity of a theory rather than the verbal definitions.

Human Technology Principle

The concept of human technology, which is also known as a training as treatment model, was first envisioned by well-known social scientist Robert Carkhuff. Carkhuff founded the Institute for Human Technology and the Human Resource Development Press in 1970. Carkhuff believes that human beings operate from three domains: physical, social/emotional, and intellectual. These domains are resources that need to be developed in people for them to be fully adaptive to their environment.

Carkhuff believes that dysfunctional or maladaptive behavior in these three domains is not due to some mysterious, intra-psychic problem within people. Rather, it is caused by a lack of skills or technical competency to function effectively in society.

Carkhuff also believes that people are not intrinsically bad or crazy. They are unskilled and this makes them maladaptive. They are unskilled because no one has taken the time to teach the "technology" of how to be a human being "physically," "socially/emotionally," or "intellectually."

Carkhuff challenges the belief, held in many academic circles, that most human dysfunction is intrinsic or genetic. Carkhuff thinks that every aspect of human functions should be treated as a technical competency problem. His belief is that people have to be taught how to relate, emote, think, and take care of their physical bodies by being *shown*, not by simply being *told* (Carkhuff & Berenson, 1977).

Are we too reliant on words in describing leadership?

There have been several excellent and popular books on leadership such as John Maxwell's *The 21 Irrefutable Laws of Leadership;* Stephen Covey's *The Seven Habits of Highly Effective People;* Ken Blanchard's, et al., *Leadership and the One Minute Manager;* Sheldon Bowles' *Gung Ho;* and Dale Carnegie's *The Leader in You.*

The problem with these books and other books on leadership or books in general is their reliance on words. Why might this be a problem?

There is no doubt that spoken and written language as a form of technology plays a significant role in our progressive evolving as social beings. It increases our ability to move knowledge and information tenfold among human kind. This is probably why IQ tests place such a heavy emphasis on linguistic ability as a form of intelligence.

The problem with words is they often distort reality rather than describe it. In S. I. Hayakawa's (former president of San Francisco State College) 1958 *Saturday Evening Post* article entitled "How Words Change Our Lives," he describes this problem succinctly:

> If one stops to think for a moment, it is clear that to define a word, as a dictionary does, is simply to explain the word with more words. To be thorough about defining, we should next have to define the words used in the definition, then define the words used in defining the words used in the definition ... and so on. Defining words with

more words, in short, gets us at once into what mathematicians call an "infinite regress." Alternatively, it can get us into the kind of runaround we sometimes encounter when we look up "impertinence" and find it defined as "impudence," so we look up "impudence" and find it defined as "impertinence." Yet—and here we come to another common reaction pattern—people often act as if words can be explained fully with more words. To a person who asked for a definition of jazz, Louis Armstrong is said to have replied, "Man, when you got to ask what it is, you'll never get to know," proving himself to be an intuitive semanticist as well as a great trumpet player (Hayakawa, 1958).

The danger of using words is the "infinite regress" they can create. Watching political debates is often painful because the politicians get into a war of words (infinite regress) and one wonders if anything has been or will be accomplished. Another problem with words, especially if they are abstract or conceptual, is how they are translated into actions and the problems that occur.

Leadership books like those listed above try to get around this by providing checklists, steps, habits, and laws that make the practice of leadership less conceptual. The problem with this approach is that the checklists, steps, habits, and laws are not defined in actionable terms. For example, how does the reader know when he or she has met the criteria of "how to respect" as well as "what does it look like" in measurable and quantifiable terms? Many of these checklists, steps, habits, and laws use catch-phrases like the "law of magnetism" and "spirit of the squirrel." This certainly helps the reader remember the leader concepts, but how do you measure magnetism by humans in actionable and measurable terms? Is magnetism measured by physical attractiveness, dress, tone of voice, or the degree of eye contact utilized? Despite the catchy phrases and jargon, these approaches are still conceptual or abstract.

Robert Mager has written several books that address the problem of words being translated into action. In his book *Goal Analysis,* he explores this problem by telling the following story:

Once upon a time in the land of Fuzz, King Aling called his cousin Ding and commanded, "Go ye out into all of Fuzzland and find me the goodest of men, whom I shall reward for his goodness."

"But how will I know when I see one?" asked the Fuzzy.

"Why, he will be *sincere,*" scoffed the King, and whacked off a leg for his impertinence.

So, the Fuzzy limped out to find a good man. But soon he returned, confused and empty-handed.

"But how will I know one when I see one?" he asked again.

"Why, he will be *dedicated,*" grumbled the King, and whacked off another leg for his impertinence.

So the Fuzzy hobbled away once more to look for the goodest of men. But again he returned, confused and empty-handed.

"But how will I know one when I see one?" he pleaded.

"Why, he will have *internalized his growing awareness,*" fumed the King, and whacked off another leg for his impertinence.

So the Fuzzy, now on his last leg, hopped out to continue his search. In time, he returned with the wisest, most sincere and dedicated Fuzzy in all of Fuzzland, and stood him before the King.

"Why, this man won't do at all," roared the King. "He is much too thin to suit me." Whereupon, he whacked off the last leg of the Fuzzy, who fell to the floor with a squishy thump (Mager, 1972).

The moral to the above story is that our interpretations of words like *sincere, dedicated,* and *internalized growing awareness* mean different things to different people in terms of what they look like.

Technologizing Leaders: Words into Action

We need to move to a leadership technology in developing our leaders of the future. Concepts such as *courage, integrity, foresight,* etc., that we use to describe leaders need to be validated in a way that makes them quantifiable. And when these concepts are quantifiable, we can begin to measure their validity as concepts we want to replicate in leaders of the future. Consider the following scenario:

Making the Point

Susan Smith is a candidate for a key customer service management position in an organization. One of the criteria for success in this new position is a social competency test called "Listening Skills Ability."

The first question on the test is "How do you know good listening ability when you see it?" (A behavior factor in listening skills is auditory memory capacity.)

Ms. Smith's listening skills can be measured by operationalizing several scenarios that require her to demonstrate her auditory memory.

Ms. Smith is given a test where she is presented with five video-simulated scenarios. These scenarios are presented on a screen where different people make 60-second statements to Ms. Smith.

Following each 60-second scenario, Ms. Smith is asked to report back what she heard. Her responses are tape recorded and transcribed. They are then rated in terms of their percentage of accuracy with what she heard in the five video simulations.

The established cut-off point for listening ability is 70% or above accuracy. Ms. Smith receives a score of 74% accuracy based on what she heard. She has passed that listening competency.

Even if Ms. Smith were not to pass that listening competency, but she passed others to a point that meets hiring standards, she could be trained to be a better listener.

The above example does two things: it operationalizes listening ability, which also allows it to be measured. The operationalizing and measuring meet the validation criteria that P. W. Bridgman felt was so critical.

By technologizing leadership, we create the ability to validate the concepts of leadership, such as being a good listener. Leadership is now becoming science versus an art.

In subsequent chapters, we will begin technologizing leadership and the six human dimensions necessary to be a complete leader. We will have to use words, though we know the potential for faulty application of words into actions.

At the end of each chapter, a self-administered technical assessment will be presented. These assessments will give you a rough estimate of your technical competency in that dimension, though the validity of these assessments can be increased by asking several people who know you to anonymously fill these assessments out regarding your technical proficiency.

References

Carkhuff, R. R., & Berenson, B. G. (1977). *Beyond counseling and therapy*. New York: Holt, Rinehart and Winston.

Collins, F. S. (2006). *The language of God: A scientist presents evidence for belief* (pp. 5–6). New York: Free Press.

Greenspan, A. (2007). *The age of turbulence: Adventures in a new world* (pp. 142–163). New York: Penguin Press.

John Wooden Biography—Academy of Achievement. (2010, June 21). *Academy of Achievement Main Menu*. Retrieved June 25, 2010, from http://www.achievement.org/autodoc/page/woo0bio-1

Hayakawa, S. I. (1958). How words change our lives. *Saturday Evening Post*.

Isaacson, W. (2007). *Einstein: his life and universe*. New York: Simon & Schuster.

Mager, R. F. (1972). *Goal analysis*. Belmont, CA: Fearon.

WGBH American Experience. (n.d.) Jonestown: The life and death of Peoples Temple. Introduction. PBS: Public Broadcasting Service. Retrieved January 13, 2010, from http://www.pbs.org/wgbh/american experience/features/introduction/jonestown-introduction/

Wikipedia. (n.d.). Enron scandal. *Wikipedia, the free encyclopedia*. Retrieved January 13, 2010, from http://en.wikipedia.org/wiki/Enron-scandal

Chapter 2

Physicality Dimension

> "Beauty is a greater recommendation than any letter of recommendation."
>
> > – Aristotle
>
> "But bless us things may be lovable that are not altogether handsome—I hope."
>
> > – George Eliot

Physicality is probably the most basic human attribute that affects our perceptions of others and our willingness to let them lead or influence us.

Physicality is defined as the physical presence a person has. It can be measured in terms of physical attractiveness, height, weight, masculinity, and body movement. It is also reflected in one's skin health and complexion, hair texture, eye size and color, nose shape and size, lip shape and size, body size and symmetry.

For example, the term *leading man* in movies reflects the power of physicality. In movies, leading men who are short in stature but have attractive faces and body builds are made to look taller. This is done by utilizing camera angles, lifts in shoes, and shorter co-stars to accentuate the belief that tallness represents power. Army generals, for example, are rarely short in stature according to research studies. For many years, height requirements were utilized in police hiring policies.

There is also the association with body muscularity and movement as indicative of power and influence. Amateur and professional athletes are revered in many societies. They are frequently used in modern societies in advertising to promote products, in public service announcements, and in promoting political candidates and issues.

Athletes are often granted powers and abilities beyond their physical skills. They are portrayed as role models for the complete person even when they lack some of the other human attributes discussed in this book such as intellectuality, sociability, emotionality, and morality.

The current power of physicality is probably a by-product of our early ancestors where physical strength, guile, and appearance of health determined survival of the fittest. Hunter-gatherer tribes, for instance, did and still do require physicality as the critical aspect of longevity. The mental, social, emotional, and moral attributes of humans, although important in early human evolution (from the caves to the executive suites), were not as critical. Contemporary human societies have gone through three successive phases since our hunter/gatherer origins. They are agricultural, industrial, and now informational societies. The newest phase "informational" has spawned a greater human need for intellectual, social, emotional, and moral competencies.

The physicality dimension is now much broader in our modern world and needs to be acknowledged as a leadership dimension.

The physicality dimension in this book is defined as one's ability to maintain the physical body's appearance, health, and utilization. Despite the evolutionary necessity for advancement in the previous five dimensions, the physicality dimension has also progressed. Life expectancies are much higher in industrialized nations. Physicality concerns beyond physical strength and stamina are now being promoted. Many contemporary societies now stress hygiene, nutrition, and physical appearance.

Let's discuss some of the facts related to physicality.

Fact 1: Physical attractiveness matters.

Physical attractiveness is a powerful influence or authority. Currently it has lost importance in our culture, at least in terms of public correctness, to seek physical beauty. It is seen as being vain. It is trivialized in terms of its true value to human existence: "beauty is only skin deep," "never judge a book by its cover," "beauty is in the eye of the beholder," etc. Paul Newman, the actor, was quoted as saying, "To work as hard as I have worked, to accomplish anything, and then have some yo-yo come up and say, 'Take off those dark glasses and let's have a look at those blue eyes,' is really discouraging."

There is no doubt that beauty on the outside may not reflect beauty on the inside. In Nancy Etcoff's book *Survival of the Prettiest*, she states that "any reading of psychology or anthropology texts written before the late 1960's would suggest that physical appearance has absolutely no bearing on human attitudes or affections and no human role in human mental life" (2000).

Despite the tendency to minimize the power of physical attractiveness, it is hardwired like our addiction to fast food. It is documented that infants gaze longer at attractive faces than unattractive faces. It is well established that beauty preference operates at an unconscious level and is not learned. Billions of dollars are spent on cosmetics and plastic surgery.

Our fear of attractiveness is justified. Attractiveness can have social ramifications such as sexual harassment and discrimination against those who are not attractive from a biological standpoint. It frequently lessens the value of inner beauty of people. The inner beauty of a first-rate intellect, temperament, and character may not be seen or appreciated because of it.

Physicality is the ability to be physically attractive beyond the biological givens. It is the ability to take what you have physically and work those physical attributes that are malleable such as grooming, physical fitness, and hygiene.

Fact 2: Physical attractiveness is hardwired into our nature.

It appears that attractiveness may be more about nature versus nurture. In other words, what we find physically attractive may not be only a learned behavior.

For instance infants will maintain a longer gaze toward an attractive face based on symmetry of the face. A symmetric face is well-proportioned in terms of eyes, eye placement, mouth shape and placement, as well as nose shape and placement. Of course that infant's gaze may change based on the facial expression the child sees (Maurer & Barrera, 1981).

David Buss found in a survey of 37 cultures (he interviewed over 10,000 people between the ages of 14 and 70) that although kindness was a universal sign of attractiveness, physical attractiveness and health were the most important factors in choosing a mate. This was more prevalent, Buss found, among cultures where physical health and attractiveness were affected by physical diseases (Buss, 1989). In essence, health and attractiveness were valued more because they were qualities that were easily attainable—disease, poor nutrition, and lack of medicine often put attractiveness out of reach for most.

It appears we are drawn to physically attractive people, and this attraction may enable them to influence us.

Fact 3: You are what you eat.

The recent emphasis on nutrition and physicality has been a long time coming. The science behind nutrition has grown rapidly. With any science, you can get conflicting results about what to eat and not to eat. There is no doubt that what you ingest has a profound effect on every aspect of your well-being.

In 1992, the USDA (United States Department of Agriculture) published a food pyramid to graphically represent its guidelines for healthy eating. Revisions were published in 2005 and again in 2010. Both revisions emphasize more grains and place a heavy emphasis on exercise. The problem with the 2005 version, according to some nutrition experts, is that it did not address more attention on the dangers of sugar and some types of fats and the benefits of certain oils. For more information please see, "The Report of the Dietary Guidelines Advisory Committee on Dietary Guidelines for Americans, 2005" at www.health.gov/dietaryguidelines/dga2005/report.

While the 2010 version, called MyPyramid, emphasizes a more "individualized approach" to making healthy eating choices and incorporating exercise, critics question whether the recommendations will affect real change in how Americans make dietary choices.

Nutritionists are now proposing another food pyramid that encourages the consumption of healthy fats and whole grain foods but stresses minimal use of butter, red meat, and refined carbohydrates.

The new suggested pyramid still stresses daily exercise and consumption of whole grains as essential but has added oils such as olive, canola, soy, corn, sunflower, peanut, and other vegetable oils. It also suggests, as in the past, that vegetables be eaten in abundance and fruit at least two to three servings per day. Nuts and legumes are important sources of protein, as are fish, poultry, and eggs, according to the pyramid. The USDA also suggests that alcohol, in moderation, is acceptable.

The 2005 dietary guidelines, which remained in effect until the 2010 dietary guidelines were published, were based on disease rates' correlation with food consumption. The Nurses' Health Study tracked 67,271 women and 38,615 men in the health professions and found that those who followed the "new" (2005) food pyramid recommendations had significantly lower rates of cardiovascular disease. The study also found there was significant impact on food intake and cancer rates (The Nurses' Health Study, www.channing.harvard.edu/nhs/).

There will be more discussion on nutrition science later in this chapter.

Fact 4: The more you move, the longer you live.

It appears that in American society the need for physical movement has lessened due to technology that enables people to reduce physical exertion. Technology such as the automobile, riding lawnmowers, escalators, and even drive-thru's at fast food restaurants has minimized the use of the human body. This, coupled with the rising obesity problem, has created serious health problems from diabetes to cardiac diseases. The term *couch potato* reflects this change in the utilization of physical body movement to survive.

Jeremy N. Morris, a British epidemiologist, compared heart attack rates among double-decker bus drivers and conductors in the late 1940s and early 1950s which laid the groundwork for current aerobic fitness science. In 1949, Morris began tracking the heart attack rates of hundreds of drivers and conductors. He found the drivers sat 90 percent of the time during their shifts, while the conductors (collecting tickets) climbed about 600 steps per shift. Morris then found that the heart attack rate among the conductors was about half that of the drivers. In a follow-up to the original conductor-driver study, Morris found that other factors such as body type were not related to heart attacks. It appeared physical movement was the predictor.

To further corroborate his research, Morris did studies with mail delivery workers. He found that the mail delivery workers who rode bicycles or walked had far fewer heart attacks than clerks sitting behind windows or at desks. Morris later did studies in the 1960s regarding the physical activity of 18,000 men in sedentary civil service jobs. The ones who exercised aerobically reduced their heart attacks by half. For a review of Dr. Morris's work, please see Paffenbarger, Blair & Lee, 2001. Coincidently, Jeremy Morris lived until he was 99 years old.

The phrase "move it or lose it" now has validity.

Fact 5: Physical fitness can improve mental and emotional health.

In our current information technology world, we are forgetting that we were wired to be physically active. The tech world typically requires mental activity only. This mental-activity-only situation causes us to not move our heart rate and lungs sufficiently to move necessary amounts of oxygen and blood flow to the brain.

The brain needs sufficient oxygen and blood flow to increase many of the brain chemicals necessary for thinking and emotional control. For example, exercise increases the brain chemical serotonin, a known neurotransmitter related to emotional well-being. Low levels of serotonin have been related to depression and poor anger management. Two other brain chemicals, norepinephrine and dopamine, are increased by exercise. They are needed for the moving of our thoughts and emotions. Moving our muscles produces proteins that travel through the blood and play a huge role in higher thought processes. These proteins are called insulin growth factor (IGF-1) and vascular endothelial growth factor (VEGF).

In John Ratey's book *Spark,* he discussed numerous studies that connect the criticality of physical fitness and mental well-being. Ratey summarizes the following as the benefits of exercise in terms of mental and emotional well-being:

1. Exercise could be the single-most powerful tool to optimize brain power. It does this by increasing neurotransmitters and neurotrophic factors released from muscles, which then build new capillaries in the brain necessary for more flexible brain connections.

2. Exercise reduces obesity, and obesity doubles the chances of dementia.

3. Exercise increases your ability to tolerate stress. High levels of stress increase cortisol levels that can cause the onset of dementia and depression.

4. Exercise increases your ability to manage your moods. Mood problems can cause problems in relationships that can cause social isolation.

5. Exercise boosts the immune system functioning. Stress and aging depress the immune system. Exercise rallies antibodies in the immune system that attack bacterial and viral infections. A healthy immune system also activates cells that fix damaged tissue, lowering inflammation in the body.

6. Exercise can boost motivation. Without motivation, the reasons for living are not there. Your body will be busy living if it is moving and busy dying if it is not.

7. Exercise fosters brain plasticity (flexibility), which helps the brain to be active and better prepared to handle any damage it might experience due to disease or trauma (Ratey & Hagerman, 2008).

The bottom line is that you were born to use your body physically as well as mentally. By not using your body, you are going against what nature intended for you to be healthy physically, mentally, and emotionally.

Fact 6: Grooming and the maintenance of physical appearance matters.

Grooming involves the cleaning and tidying up of one's appearance. Humans have developed a whole industry of professional hairdressers, barbers, manicurists, and pedicurists to help us with our grooming.

Grooming may be hardwired into our nature. It appears to be in the nature of many of our domesticated animals, such as cats and dogs, who lick their fur as a form of grooming. It is highly practiced in our closest ancestors; primates such as monkeys and great apes are frequently seen grooming themselves and each other by carefully picking parasites and dirt from each other's bodies.

Grooming in humans goes even further in the cleaning, cutting, and styling of hair. Humans also groom their skin in terms of washing, shaving, and using lotions. Whitening and straightening teeth are also seen in humans as signs of good hygiene.

The use of cosmetics and toiletries is a $45 billion industry, especially in North America, Europe, and Japan. In 1996, a study reported that 88 percent of women over 18 said they had used color cosmetics in the past six months.

Grooming also appears to be a by-product of socioeconomic status due to its expense and time consumption. Consequently, it may reflect levels of status. Status reflects a person's rank, social position, relation to others, and importance. For this reason, the grooming of a person can influence others.

An interesting aspect of grooming is humans' management of their body hair. For women, other than the hair on their head, body hair can be seen as offensive in many cultures. It is therefore removed. Women naturally have less body hair than men, but in many cultures, they remove what they have. You will not see a supermodel with hairy legs.

Many men in Western culture are more likely to consider hair removal than in the past. It is not likely you will see a male body builder with body hair. There has only been one actor who portrayed "Tarzan" in movies who had body hair. His name was Mike Henry. On the other hand, a male can have hair on his legs and arms, which accentuates his masculinity.

A recent trend in male hair is to remove all hair from the head when baldness starts to occur. It appears that it is more acceptable to have a great deal of hair or none at all than to have a quantity of hair that falls between the two extremes. The absence of hair on the male head also exaggerates the appearance of strength because the head looks smaller against the neck and shoulders.

Another major aspect of grooming is maintaining skin. When we are young, skin for most of us is fresh and alive—it is in bloom. As aging occurs, our skin gradually loses its softness and glow. Our skin starts to break down, becoming drier, less supple, and less elastic. The crinkling of our skin that used to go away now becomes permanent and wrinkled. Fair-skinned Caucasians become wrinkled 10 to 20 years earlier than African-Americans, and women tend to wrinkle before men.

But aging is not the only problem. Bad health habits can make it worse. Smoking and too much exposure to the sun can age skin rapidly. To counter this, cosmetic surgery has become rampant. Nearly half of all cosmetic surgeries are in America. Plastic surgery is now as commonplace as dyeing one's hair. Seventy percent of cosmetic patients earn less than $50,000 and 30 percent below $25,000.

It appears skin maintenance is critical to our being perceived as youthful and healthy and is reflective of our status.

Fact 7: Body geometry matters.

Geometry is the mathematical study of the properties and relationship between points, lines, surfaces, and solids. There appears to be an innate attraction cross-culturally to human bodies that are geometrically proportional. This is also referred to as body symmetry. The word *fecundity* is often associated with the human body and face that are physically balanced or orderly because the word implies fertility or fruitfulness.

Physical symmetry is important because it indicates overall fitness in other animals as well as humans. Asymmetry may be a critical indicator of a body's inability to cope with nature's adversities, namely parasites, inbreeding, pollutants, difficult habitats, and other stressors.

Two scientists—Ander Møller, a zoologist, and Randy Thornhill, a behavioral ecologist—conducted a review of 62 studies of 41 animal species. They found that fluctuating asymmetry was associated with mating success and sexual attractiveness in 78 percent of species, including humans (Møller & Thornhill, 1998).

Male body symmetry offers distinct advantages. Men with symmetrical bodies report that they start having sex three or four years earlier than men who do not and have two to three times as many partners. Research has found that men with symmetrical width of even their feet, ankles, elbows, hands, wrists, and ears are more attractive than those with asymmetrical width to women (Thornhill & Gangestad, 1994). It has also been found that asymmetrical men are more faithful and invest more in their relationship than symmetrical men (Thornhill & Gangestad, 1994). This may be due to the fact that symmetrical men are favored by women and may have more sexual partners from which to choose.

Symmetry in women is also favored by men. Symmetrical women have more sexual partners than asymmetrical women. A huge factor in women's symmetrical attractiveness is the waist-to-hip ratio. Psychologist Devandra Singh looked at men's perception of body shape in 18 cultures. He concluded that waist-to-hip ratio is often more important than breast size and weight. Singh also found that men overwhelmingly chose women of average weight but who had a 0.7 waist-to-hip ratio. Singh concluded that men have an innate preference for female bodies that have narrow waists and full hips, which signal high estrogen and fertility and low testosterone. Singh researched Miss America pageant winners from the 1920s through the 1980s as well as *Playboy* magazine models, and found that waist-to-hip ratio for Miss America varied only 0.69 to 0.72 and *Playboy* models 0.68 to 0.71 (Singh, 1993).

Another factor in body geometry and attractiveness is facial symmetry. This involves the placement and shape of the eyes, nose, mouth, and chin. Donald Giddon, a lecturer at Harvard School of Dental Medicine, developed a computer program that displays a face in profile. The program allows the user to create facial features that are acceptable and more pleasing to them. What Giddon found is that perceptions of facial attraction changed significantly with minor changes to facial features. He found, for example, that one millimeter of change in a facial feature changed the observer's view from pleasing to very unpleasing (Giddon, Bernier, Kinchen, & Evans, 1996).

Overall, it appears that age and gender have little effect on perceptions of facial beauty. A study conducted by Cross noted that three-month-old babies gaze longer at faces that adults find attractive. Cross also found that 7-year-olds, 12-year-olds, 17- year-olds, and adults did not differ in their ratings of attractiveness of the faces. Men and women also agreed when it comes to judging attractiveness in men and women even though they will only admit it anonymously (Cross & Cross, 1971).

It also appears that when different cultures—Australia, Austria, England, China, India, Japan, Korea, Switzerland, and the United States—were analyzed in terms of their perceptions, there was universal agreement about which faces were beautiful (Cross & Cross, 1971).

A study by Jones and Hill addresses perceptions of facial attractiveness in five cultures—Brazilian, U.S., Russian, Hiwi, and Ache Indians. The researchers found there was significant agreement among the five cultures in their beauty rating with some subtle differences. They found there was universal agreement in the five cultures with regard to geometric proportions of the face. The five cultures liked female faces with small lower faces (small jaws and relatively small chins) and eyes that were large in relation to the length of the face (Jones, 1995).

It appears that the geometric body has some universal attractiveness factors that different ages, races, cultures, and genders agree upon. Some of these we cannot control due to genetics, but we nevertheless attempt to in contemporary society through cosmetic surgery. There are others we have control of, depending on our willingness to continually work at maintaining what we do have geometrically through exercise and nutrition.

Fact 8: What we cover our bodies with matters.

All cultures deal with covering their bodies in varying degrees. This obviously is dependent on one's culture, environment, climate, values, needs, and types of activities. "Covering" not only includes clothes; it includes ornaments, jewelry, and make-up.

The writer George Orwell once said, "You may have three half-pence in your pocket and not a prospect in the world... but in your new clothes you can stand on a street corner, indulging in a daydream of yourself as Clark Gable or Greta Garbo."

The coverings we use are important because they often reflect the possible social status of a person or the social status they desire to be but may not be. On the other hand, the use of a uniform is to do the opposite. The uniform in the military or police work and other professions is to make people look alike or like they belong to a specific group. Of course with a uniform, ornaments such as insignia, badges, and medals are used to show a separation in rank or status (Payne, Winakor, & Farrell-Beck, 1992).

Thorstein Veblen, an economist in the late 1800s and early 1900s, wrote a book called *The Theory of the Leisure Class*. In it Veblen analyzed how people used clothes to state a social position. One of his most famous terms was "conspicuous consumption," which basically stated that the amassing of valuable things, including clothing and jewelry, reflected high status lifestyles (Veblen, 1912).

Clothing not only attempts to show our status; it is often used to accentuate our bodies to increase physical attraction despite its covering of body parts. Clothing is often used to accentuate trimmer waists, broader shoulders, larger breasts, and muscular arms. In J. C. Flügel's book, *The Psychology of Clothes*, he discusses how clothing is selectively designed to offer what he called "shifting erogenous zones" (Flügel, 1930). Ornaments such as beads, gemstones, necklaces, rings, earrings, watches, bracelets, and ribbons are also used to accentuate social status along with clothing.

A major concept in covering is fashion, which refers to a current or popular custom or style, especially in the way one dresses. The fashion industry is huge, and many colleges offer degrees in fashion design. Some historians date the birth of fashion to 14th century Europe (Etcoff, 2000). Until then, people tended to wear what earlier generations wore.

Historians linked the emergence of fashion to the new monetary power of the 14th century. Businessmen, bankers, and merchants wanted strict demarcations of wealth and status. Fashion created a visible sign of wealth and social aspirations.

Another aspect of covering is cosmetics, which are primarily used by women to emphasize their attractiveness. Lipstick, eye make-up, and rouge are all used to highlight facial beauty (Etcoff, 2000).

Fact 9: Hygiene is important to not only physical health but physical attractiveness.

Hygiene is defined as the principles of maintaining one's health and is sometimes referred to as sanitary science. There is no doubt that hygiene is critical to our survival in terms of controlling bacteria and viruses that can cause illness. It could be argued that hygiene is one of the most important scientific discoveries in medicine.

In Virginia Smith's book, *Clean: A History of Personal Hygiene and Purity* (2007), she says the origins of modern views regarding cleanliness can be traced from the ancient Mesopotamians to current grooming habits such as baths, manicures, and hairstyling. Smith further advocates that the maintenance of a clean outward appearance plays a central role in sexual attraction. Smith also adds that there is opposition to this view in many circles due to psychological and religious beliefs that *inner* purity or cleanliness should be valued more than *outer* cleanliness.

In William Miller's book, *The Anatomy of Disgust* (1998), he states that there is nothing like skin gone bad; it is in fact the marring of skin that makes up much of the substance of the ugly and monstrous. It must be noted that a regular sight in the Middle Ages was skin that oozed pus or had sores or skin lesions since many citizens had the inability to develop the hygienic practices that deterred these problems. On the other hand, the belief that people whose outward appearance reflects their inner appearance could be called into question.

In his book *The Human Zoo* (1969), Desmond Morris, a zoologist, says that not only flawless skin is a worldly desire, but flowing, healthy hair is as well. The look and management of one's hair is highly stressed in many cultures as a sign of physical health and attractiveness. Baldness, unkempt facial hair, or ungroomed hair, at least in the Western world, is viewed by many as a sign of poor grooming and therefore poor hygiene and health.

Body odor is also a sign of one's perceived hygiene in many societies. Natural body odor is often considered repulsive, hence the frequent use of deodorant by those in Western cultures. In other cultures, someone's natural odor is a sign of identification and attractiveness. On the other hand, many

Western women report that they enjoy wearing a man's T-shirt or sleeping on his pillow when the man is absent so that his presence can be detected.

Most of the scientific research on smell regarding humans has been done with women. It appears women have a keener sense of smell that is at its height during puberty. In research conducted by Claus Wedekind (1997), women were more attracted to men who smell least like them, but were more attracted to men who smelled more like them while on birth control pills (Wedekind & Furi, 1997). It appears that when we interfere with reproductive capability, we affect women's attraction to men based on smell.

Given these examples, it seems as though hygiene is an important factor in physical attraction from a variety of perspectives.

Fact 10: Men and women perceive physicality in different ways.

How a male looks is important in terms of power and dominance. Allan Mazur, in a study of West Point cadets, found that facial structure affected rank in junior and senior years at the academy. He found that what could be described as handsome, wide, and rectangular faces predicted rank attainment in the academy and later military career attainment. Mazur also found that handsome cadets who did not perform well academically predicted failure in their careers after the academy. It seems as though the external appearance coupled with internal ability, i.e., academic intelligence, was the best predictor of rank in the military (Mueller and Mazur, 1996).

Women value male physicality, but not to the extent that men value female physicality. In Nancy Etcoff's book mentioned earlier, a woman makes her initial evaluation of a man's physicality in terms of looks, but this can change as she looks more closely at him. Many women take a longer look beyond physicality. Their choice of man is more than fertility—it is about the man's ability to help her with a child in terms of protection, resources, and helpfulness (Etcoff, 2000).

John Townsend, an anthropologist, showed pictures of men and women to other men and women. The pictures ranged from very attractive men and women to below-average looking. The participants were asked which individuals they could see themselves being with intimately based on the pictures and socio-economic status. The women preferred the best looking men with the most money. The women then selected the average-looking and below-average looking men who had money versus attractive males with no money. It appears as though social status means a great deal.

Men, on the other hand, preferred attractive women only. Unattractive women were not considered, even when they had status or money (Townsend & Levy, 1990). Men seemed preoccupied with women's physicality in terms of attraction and influence. They may also defer to men's physicality as evidenced in Mazur's study at West Point with cadets selected to lead junior and senior classes.

Women do value physicality in males, and this is likely a by-product of our history when physicality in hunter-gatherer tribes was everything in terms of survival. The physical male provided females with the best chance of survival for herself and her offspring.

It would seem, then, that women in modern society value physicality, but not so much in terms of physical appearance. The critical variable for women appears to be the amount of power or status a man has. Physicality can reflect a type of power but in modern society, power can be reflected in one's intellectual and social resources.

Developing and Applying your Physicality

Physical Fitness Dimension

"The more physically fit you are, the more resilient your brain becomes. Exercise could be the single most powerful tool to optimize brain power."

— John Ratey, *Spark*

This dimension measures a person's overall muscle strength and his or her muscle, ligament, and tendon flexibility, as well as cardio-respiratory endurance and efficiency.

Muscle strength can be measured in basically two ways: dynamic and static. Dynamic strength, sometimes called moving strength, is the ability to maintain muscle strength for a period of time and has to do with things like the number of pushups, pull ups, sit ups, etc., one can do without feeling fatigue. It can also be determined by the number of repetitions one can do in different weight lifting exercises such as presses, curls, deep knee bends, etc.

Static strength is sometimes referred to as explosive strength. It is based on how much muscle strength one has in one movement versus several movements as in dynamic strength. It can be measured by how much weight one can handle in one repetition or movement, e.g., the highest amount of weight a person can bench press or leg press.

The flexibility dimension measures the degree one can stretch a muscle, ligament, or tendon without straining or tearing it. It is sometimes referred to as elasticity. Muscles are compressed when dealing with resistant force or objects. Muscles, ligaments, and tendons can be strained or torn if they are stretched too far or if the body moves in an unfamiliar direction. The best way to strengthen one's flexibility of muscles, tendons, and ligaments is stretching or yoga.

Cardio-respiratory efficiency and endurance is the body's ability to coordinate oxygen and blood flow throughout the body in a balanced manner, especially when the body is moving. Cardio-respiratory function requires healthy heart and lung functioning so that blood flow and oxygen is evenly distributed. It is usually determined by measuring one's heart rate before, during, and following physical exertion.

Cardiologists measure an individual's cardio-respiratory efficiency and endurance with treadmill tests. Efficiency is the ability of the body to move blood and oxygen throughout the body with minimal strain to the body. Endurance is the heart's and lungs' ability to maintain movement over time. The most common way to measure one's cardio-respiratory efficiency *and* endurance is jogging. The distance one can run is the endurance dimension where the time it takes to run that distance would indicate efficiency dimension.

There are other fitness measurement dimensions such as Body Mass Index, sometimes referred to as BMI. BMI is the ratio of body fat to muscle. The more muscle one has compared to fat, the more physically fit they are likely to be. BMI is usually measured by what is called height to weight ratio, but this is not necessarily the most accurate way. One might have the right weight for their height, but his or her muscles may still be under-strengthened or toned due to a lack of exertion.

A person who has exemplified this dimension is Jillian Michaels.

Jillian Michaels—Personal Trainer

Jillian Michaels was an overweight child. She once stated that when she was 12 years old, she weighed 175 pounds and was 5 feet tall. When she was 13 years old, her mother enrolled her in a martial arts class. This was the turning point for Michaels. Since then she has dedicated her life to help people lose weight and be their physical best. She continued with martial arts for the next 17 years and has a black belt in both Akarui-Do and Muay Thai.

Michaels became a personal trainer and is now very well known to the public, making guest appearances on the ABC television show *The Doctors* and being one of the trainers on the NBC television show *The Biggest Loser.*

Michaels uses a combination of strength training techniques with her clients, including Pilates, plyometrics, kickboxing, yoga, and weight training.

While working with *The Biggest Loser* franchise, Michaels has released numerous fitness books and DVDs. She has also worked with eDiets.com to produce a meal plan for health-conscious people called "The Jillian Michaels Meal Delivery Plan." Michaels is a celebrity adviser to National Day of Dance for Heart Health, an organization that encourages people to make exercise fun and to laugh, learn, and dance to a healthier heart.

Jillian Michaels co-owns the Sky Sport & Spa in Los Angeles and Empowered Media. In 2008, Michaels worked with Nintendo Wii to release a new video game called "Jillian Michaels Fitness Ultimatum 2009" (www. wikipedia.org/jillianmichaels, www.jillianmichaels.org).

Nutritional Dimension

> "Eating healthy foods was extremely important to people of earlier eras, perhaps even more important than it is today."
>
> – Rachel Landau, *Scientific American Reports*

The cliché "you are what you eat" best sums up the nutritional dimensions. The type and amount of food people consume affect their physicality in many ways.

Many human-made foods contain ingredients that are not natural for our systems to consume. One such ingredient is artificial preservatives, which are utilized to preserve the shelf-life of foods and decrease the risk of spoilage. The long-term and even short-term effects of some of these preservatives, all of which are foreign to our body's natural intake rules, probably present problems.

Modern foods also utilize artificial flavorings to positively stimulate our taste sensors so that we want to consume them. Soft drinks and snack foods are two products in which these are found. They have very little nutritional value; they primarily satisfy our immediate feelings of hunger but are typically laden with sugar, fat, and sodium. These foods are sometimes referred to as "empty calories" because they are calorie-dense but offer few benefits.

There are also foods that contain nutrients that our bodies need but not in the amounts our bodies actually require. For example, our bodies require certain levels of sodium (salt) to function properly, but many foods contain high levels of salt, thus causing many of us to ingest too much. Salt is found in many foods because it can act as a preservative and provides a pleasurable taste.

Glucose, a type of simple carbohydrate, is also a common natural ingredient that our body needs for energy. Unfortunately, much of our glucose needs are met through the consumption of sugar. Our bodies naturally seek out the sweet taste of sugar because we associate it with foods that boost our energy. We are wired to seek sweet tastes just like we seek salt because our bodies tell us we need it. Unfortunately, just like salt, many foods contain sugar, and we consume too much of it. The most obvious high-sugar foods are candy, pastries, and often many of the desserts we consume. These foods have very little nutritional value and again could be called empty calories in terms of nutritional value.

Another threat to our overall physicality is our tendency to over consume fats. We humans naturally enjoy the taste of fat based on our evolution. This is why we are attracted to fried foods and their fat content, just as we are attracted to high-sugar and salty foods. Our ancestors, especially hunter-gatherer groups, often endured long periods of time in between meals. There were no grocery stores or fast food restaurants that one could purchase food whenever they were hungry.

The reason fat tastes so good and we are drawn to it is our body's tendency to store it. We store it as a source of energy in case food is unavailable for long periods of time. In our modern world, this is not the case for many humans. This is one of the dangers of a fast food industry that perpetuates the availability of foods that contain large amounts of fat. The fact that we like fat given its taste, coupled with our natural tendency to seek it out since it is so readily available and cheaply priced in the fast food industry, contribute to our current obesity problems.

The key to nutritional fitness is the intake of non-empty calories and modifying our over-consumption of salt, sugar, and fat. The term *live food* is sometimes used to describe the foods we should ingest. Live food refers to foods that nature produces versus humans.

Examples of non-empty foods that nature produces are fresh vegetables and fruits, nuts, berries, and proteins such as fish, poultry, and meat. Of course, some of these foods that occur naturally are genetically altered to increase production and preservatives to decrease spoilage. The foods that are "purely natural" are called organic foods. These are usually more expensive due to production costs.

One of the best ways to measure one's nutritional fitness is to refer to the USDA Food Pyramid. The first food pyramid was established in 1992, and it was revised in 2005 and in 2010.

The 2010 USDA Food Pyramid recommends finding a balance between physical activity and food (MyPyramid.gov). In other words, nutrition matters, but exercise matters more.

Below are the steps of the pyramid in terms of nutritional fitness:

Most Important	1st Place	Daily Exercise/Weight Control
	2nd Place	Whole grain food and plant oil at most meals
	3rd Place	Fresh vegetables and fruits (2 to 3 servings per day)
	4th Place	Nuts and legumes (1 to 3 servings per day)
	5th Place	Fish, poultry, and eggs (0 to 2 servings per day)
	6th Place	Daily calcium supplement
Least Important	7th Place	Red meat, butter, white rice, bread, pasta, sweets

Weight control not only involves exercise, it involves careful consideration of calorie intake. One of the simplest ways to determine appropriate calorie intake is to consider the following recommendations by Thomas Lee, MD in the *Harvard Heart Letter*.

The daily target for calories is to multiply one's weight by

- 12 if you are sedentary (little/no exercise)
- 13.5 if you are somewhat active (light exercise 1 to 3 days per week)
- 15.5 if you are moderately active (moderate exercise like brisk walking 3 to 5 times per week)
- 17 if you are very active (vigorous exercise of sports 6 to 7 days per week)
- 19 if you are highly active (daily vigorous exercise or sports and a physical job)

A somewhat active male who weighs 200 pounds needs about 2,700 calories per day (200 x 13.5) to keep a steady weight.

If you want to lose weight, reduce your intake by 250 calories per day. If you keep that up for a year, you could lose 20 pounds. Make exercise activity at 15.5 level and you could lose 30 pounds.

A person who has exemplified this dimension is Jack LaLanne.

Jack LaLanne—Fitness and Nutritional Expert

Jack LaLanne ate well for as long as he had been an exercise fanatic. At 15, when he claimed sugar was literally making him crazy, his mother took him to see a speaker who preached about health and nutrition. Inspired, LaLanne completely changed his eating habits and began exercising regularly. Until he died in January 2011 at age 96, LaLanne followed the same diet and exercised two hours per day.

LaLanne claimed he had not had any refined sugar or dessert in decades. He did not eat white flour either, preferring to eat whole grains alone. Overall, his diet consisted mainly of raw vegetables—he ate 10 servings per day, as well as five servings of fresh fruit, whatever happened to be in season.

LaLanne also refrained from eating meat, poultry, or dairy; he occasionally ate fish, but preferred to eat small portions, between three and four ounces. His primary sources of protein included soy and egg whites. Beyond these limitations, LaLanne supplemented his diet with multiple vitamins and minerals.

Given these dietary preferences, it should come as no surprise that LaLanne did not consume any processed foods. To him, the reason why so many Americans are unhealthy was simple: they do not eat well. LaLanne's advise is to find out what foods are best and create a liking for them. At the end of the day, however, LaLanne said living takes hard work (Hughes, 2005).

Hygiene Dimension

"Simple 'cleanliness' I think lies at the bottom of every-thing, and seems to me to represent our animal and human side—not only the demands of our extremely ancient biology, but also our very Neolithic love of grooming orderliness and beauty."

— Virginia Smith, *Clean: A History of Personal Hygiene and Purity*

Hygiene, or hygienics, is basically science concerned with preventing illness and maintaining health. It is sometimes referred to as sanitary science or cleanliness. Terms synonymous with hygiene are *sterile, germ-free, unpolluted, uncontaminated,* or *pure.*

The maintaining of one's personal hygiene refers to the caring for one's skin, teeth, hair, eyes, ears, and nails.

Virginia Smith's book *Clean: A History of Personal Hygiene and Purity* traces the origins of modern standards of cleanliness as far back as Mesopotamia. Smith reports that the main drive behind maintaining our clean outward appearance is to increase sexual attraction. She also reports that this idea was opposed by the Christian ascetic belief that inner purity was more important (Smith, 2007).

During the Victorian era, cleanliness was linked to purity, and personal hygiene gained general consensus with the new emerging middle class in Western Europe. Smith notes in her book that we shed skin, hair, and toe- and fingernail clippings, and generally dispose of quantities of waste matter minute by minute, day by day, year in and year out—normally between three to six ounces a day, or four tons in the average lifetime. Between 75 to 80 percent of vacuum cleaner dirt consists of human skin cells (Smith, 2007).

The Greeks and Romans knew nothing of skin cells or vacuum cleaners, but they did believe in the power of a good bath. Water has always been seen as a primal necessity that transcended all cultures as having a purifying effect. Roman and Greek bath houses became masterpieces of art.

Despite the early Christian ascetic beliefs that taught against the vanity of external purity and the advocacy of internal purity, Christians eventually relented. By the Middle Ages, monasteries were the best places to find excellent baths and latrines.

In the 21st century, personal hygiene had reached general consensus in most cultures of the world according to Smith. She states in her book that for many people today there is one sole and sufficient reason for practicing personal hygiene that eclipses all others: self-presentation.

Despite the belief that hygiene is only about appearance and that it drives sexual appeal and attraction, it is obvious there is another significant reason for hygiene: disease control. In Katherine Ashenberg's book, *The Dirt on Clean: An Unsanitized History*, she notes that Americans were as filthy as their European cousins before the Civil War. What changed this was the Union army's success in controlling disease on the battlefield through hygiene (Ashenberg, 2007). This effort convinced citizens that cleanliness served more than self-presentation.

The connection between hygiene and disease control is now an accepted reason for engaging in proper hygienic practices. Below are some facts regarding the relationship between hygiene and disease control found in a 2010 *Discover Magazine* article by Liza Lentini and David Mouzon:

1. The human body is home to some thousand species of bacteria. There are more germs on your body than people in the United States.

2. Excrement dumped out of the windows into the 18th century streets contaminated the city's water supply and forced locals to drink gin instead.

3. The first toothbrush consisted of Siberian pig hair bristles wired into carved cattle bone handles and was invented in China in 1498.

4. Toothbrushing did not become routine in the United States until it was required of soldiers during World War II.

5. In 1843, Oliver Wendell Holmes campaigned for basic sanitation in hospitals, but this clashed with social ideas of the time.

6. It is believed that President James Garfield died not of a bullet wound but because the medical team that treated him had manure-stained hands and consequently caused infection.

7. The need to preserve beneficial germs is demonstrated in a study of 11,000 children that showed that an environment lacking in "good" bacteria increased the children's risk of eczema and asthma.

It can therefore be said that humans should practice hygiene fitness for two basic reasons: physical attractiveness and physical health.

A person who has exemplified this dimension is Mary Douglas.

Mary Douglas—Author

Anthropologist Mary Douglas's association with the hygiene sub-dimension is purely academic. Douglas explored the many facets of purity, both in terms of personal hygiene and religious purity in her book *Purity and Danger.*

Though Douglas's body of work has been criticized for its apparent alignment with endorsement of Catholic tradition, it has also been widely studied and analyzed (Fardon, 2007).

Known as the mother of social anthropology, Douglas was one of the first to discuss dirt as simply being matter out of place. She further suggested that our effort to get rid of dirt has everything to do with our inherent need for order (Fardon, 2007). *"Dirt is the by-product of a systematic ordering and classification of matter, in so far as ordering involves rejecting inappropriate elements,"* Douglas said.

If dirt is any matter out of place, then we naturally seek to put it in its place—away from us.

Grooming Dimension

> "No one is able to resist that delicious itch to reveal his own picture of himself through fashion."
>
> — Tom Wolfe

The lines between grooming and hygiene are often blurred because many hygiene practices affect grooming and vice versa. Washing one's face or washing one's hair, for example, improves appearance but can also improve facial skin and hair health.

There are other aspects of grooming that do not affect hygiene but are for appearance's sake only. A woman who wears makeup or a man who wears a starched button-down collared shirt with a tie is doing so for appearances only, not hygiene.

The primary goal of appearance is physical presentation of oneself. Grooming is a daily habit in many cultures. We either do it for ourselves or we procure the services of others to do it for us, e.g., hairdressers, barbers, and manicurists. Parents, up to a certain point, groom their children.

Most of our grooming involves our hair and our skin. In the United States, one study reported we spend more on grooming-type products and services than reading materials. Cosmetics and toiletries are a $45 billion industry world-wide. North America represents 30 percent of the global market, Europe 34.9 percent, Japan 18.9 percent, and other countries 16.2 percent (Francese, 1977).

Women have less body hair than men, but in many cultures what hair they do have is removed. This is done to differentiate males from females and to heighten female appeal to men. Women shave their legs, armpits, and when necessary, even facial hair so that their skin is accentuated. A woman's head hair is rarely removed and is kept groomed to improve men's attraction to her. Hair is often colored to improve appearance, mostly in females.

Face paint or makeup is used in many cultures. In the West, most males do not use makeup on their faces. This is also true in many Eastern cultures. Women conversely use face paint/makeup frequently to accentuate their faces. They may use lipstick to accentuate lips, rouge to accentuate facial skin, and eyeliner to accentuate their eyes. The use of facial paint or makeup dates back over 40,000 years in the Klasier River mouth or border regions of South Africa (Etcoff, 2000).

Clothing and jewelry are also used to accentuate one's physical presentation. Clothing as a fashion statement versus a functional need dates back to the 14th century in Europe. People with wealth and status began wearing clothing that was tailored and held together by buttons and lace to show off their physical attributes. The importance of men's clothing can be traced back to military dress. Knights' armor was fitted to the body; underneath their armor, knights wore padded garments and form-fitting stockings. This padded torso as well as the stockings remained the basis for men's clothing for centuries.

Women wore long dresses with trains that flowed behind them. The tops of their dresses had plunging necklines with welted seams that pulled at the waist to accentuate their figures. Decorations were often put on their dresses at the ends of sleeves and hems.

Historians believed that this use of fashion was linked to the new monetary power of Europe in the 14th century. Feudal society prior to the 14th century did have strict lines between wealth and status. When the feudal system ended, there was an even greater need to make this demarcation even more obvious between wealth and status. Fashion was a visible sign of prosperity and social status.

Thorstein Veblen analyzed how people used their clothes to establish social position. He used terms like *conspicuous leisure* to refer to clothing that reflected a person's ability to be leisurely and not have to worry about money or producing anything useful. This clothing might reflect high status pastimes like golf or yachting (1912).

Another area where clothing reflects power or status was a man's connection to warriors or military. Wearing trench coats, pea coats, khakis, or medals adorning a uniform reflected the power or status of these roles in society. The whole concept of a uniform is not only reflected in the military but also in law enforcement occupations and demonstrates how clothing reflects rank or status. Basically how we dress matters. This has become significantly more important in society for the past 500 years.

Conversely, the use of clothing or cosmetics to reflect power or status is often not well received by many in society. This is because the covering of our bodies allows people to conceal their true selves and perpetuate the idea that we are not equal in power or status.

During the early years of fashion, sumptuary laws were created to limit who could wear certain fabrics, widths of skirts, or lengths of shoes. The reason the sumptuary laws were created, according to sociologist Erving Goffman, was that clothing types indicated membership to a particular status group. If a person outside that group were allowed to purchase and wear certain garments, the garments would lose value as status symbols. In modern times, exorbitant pricing, rather than the use of sumptuary laws, is used to insure only the elite have access (Goffman, 1951).

A person who has exemplified this dimension is Olivia de Havilland.

Olivia de Havilland—Actress

Olivia de Havilland was a famous actress who has always played leading lady roles that required her to be the epitome of attractiveness and poise. She played alongside some of Hollywood's famous leading men such as Errol Flynn and Clark Gable.

Though Olivia de Havilland is seldom in the limelight these days, the last surviving cast member of "Gone with the Wind" is still described as vivacious and stylish as she was during her heyday 50 years ago.

Recently, French president Nicolas Sarkozy honored de Havilland with France's most prestigious accolade, the Légion d'honneur, and de Havilland looked "radiant" by all accounts. Her silver hair, swept up in a tidy bun, provided a beautiful contrast to her black gown and pearls (Eyre, 2010).

Of course, since de Havilland was an icon during Hollywood's glory days, sh was always fashionably dressed and meticulously groomed. A quick

(continued)

Internet search of de Havilland yields hundreds of photographs, mostly from the 30s, 40s, and 50s, all of which reveal her charming grace and beauty, whether the source is screen test, movie, still, or magazine cover.

Physicality Test

Let's measure your physicality potential.

Below are some actions that measure your physicality skills. Complete the statements honestly. You may want to ask some people who know you well to rate you. See how closely your score and their scores match. Don't be surprised if there is a big difference.

1. I bathe or shower

5	4	3	2	1
Every day	Every other day	As needed	Once in a while	Rarely

2. I manicure or trim my nails (fingers and toes)

5	4	3	2	1
Frequently	Often	Average amount	As needed	Rarely

3. I pay attention to changes in my body weight/waist line, etc.

5	4	3	2	1
Frequently	Often	Average amount	As needed	Rarely

4. I eat a variety of fresh fruit

5	4	3	2	1
Every day	Every other day	Twice a week	Sometimes	Rarely or not at all

5. I eat fresh vegetables

5	4	3	2	1
Every day	Every other day	Twice a week	Sometimes	Rarely or not at all

6. I walk or jog

5	4	3	2	1
Every day	3 to 4 times a week	Twice a week	Sometimes	Rarely or not at all

7. I do resistance exercises (weights, bands, isometrics, etc.)

5	4	3	2	1
3 or more times a week	Twice a week	Once a week	Sometimes	Rarely or never

8. I do flexibility exercises (stretching, etc.)

5	4	3	2	1
Every day	4 to 5 times a week	Twice a week	Sometimes	Rarely or never

9. I think it is important to dress in a way that is appropriate to the occasion.

5	4	3	2	1
Strongly agree	Agree	Moderately agree	Moderately disagree	Disagree

10. I think it is important to coordinate the clothing I wear if the situation allows or warrants it.

5	4	3	2	1
Strongly agree	Agree	Moderately agree	Moderately disagree	Disagree

Scoring:

Add your total score and multiply the total by 2. This number is your ability potential in this dimension. For example: $30 \times 2 = 60\%$ ability in this range.

A score above 80% is a good score.

A score above 90% is an excellent score.

Note: A more accurate assessment of your ability in this dimension, which consists of 40 statements/questions versus the 10 shown in this book, can be found at www.sotelligence.com.

References

Ashenburg, K. (2007). *The dirt on clean: An unsanitized history.* New York: North Point Press.

Buss, D. M. (1989). Sex differences in human mate preferences: Evolutionary hypotheses in 37 cultures. *Behavioral and Brain Sciences, 12,* 1–18.

Cross, J. F., & Cross, J. (1971). Age, sex, race, and the perception of facial beauty. *Developmental Psychology, 5*(3), 433–439. doi: 10.1037/ h0031591

Dortch, S. (1997). Women at the cosmetics counter: demographic trends in the cosmetics industry. *American demographics, 19*(3).

Etcoff, N. L. (2000). *Survival of the prettiest.* New York: Anchor books.

Eyre, H. (2010, March 19). Hollywood's sweetheart: Olivia de Havilland | Life & Style. *London News | London Evening Standard—London's newspaper.* Retrieved December 18, 2010, from http://www.thisislondon.co.uk/ lifestyle/article-23816660-hollywoods-sweetheart-olivia-de-havilland.do

Fardon, R. (2007, May 18). Obituary: Dame Mary Douglas | Education | The Guardian. *Latest news, comment and reviews from the Guardian | guardian.co.uk.* Retrieved December 17, 2010, from http://www.guardian. co.uk/news/2007/may/18/guardianobituaries.obituaries

Flügel, J. C. (1930). *The psychology of clothes.* London: Hogarth Press.

Francese, P. K. (1997). Big spenders. *American Demographics, 19*(8), 51–57.

Giddon, D. B., Bernier, D. B., Kinchen, J. A., & Evans, C. A. (1996). Comparison of two computer-animated imaging programs for quantifying facial profile preference. *Perceptual and Motor Skills, 82,* 1251–1264.

Goffman, E. (1951). Symbols of class status. *The British Journal of Sociology*, *2*(4), 294–304.

Hughes, D. (2005). Jack LaLanne interview on diet and nutrition. *Share Guide Holistic Health Magazine and Alternative Medicine Directory*. Retrieved December 18, 2010, from http://www.shareguide.com/LaLanne.html

Jillian Michaels Biography—Wikipedia. Retrieved January 8, 2011, from http://en.wikipedia.org/wiki/Jillian_Michaels_%28personal_trainer%29 | Jillian Michaels Biography. Retrieved January 8, 2011 from http://www.jillianmichaels.org/jillian-michaels-biography.php

Jones, D. (1995). Sexual selection, physical attractiveness, and facial neoteny: Cross-cultural evidence and implications. *Current Anthropology*, *36*(5), 723–748. doi: 10.1086/204427

Lentini, L., & Mouzon, D. (2007). 20 Things you didn't know about...hygiene. *Discovery Magazine*, published online 8/20/2007.

Maurer, D., & Barrera, M. (1981). Infants' perception of natural and distorted arrangements of a schematic face. *Child Development, 52*(1), 196–202. doi: 10.2307/1129230

Miller, W. I. (1998). *The anatomy of disgust*. Cambridge, MA: Harvard University Press.

Møller, A., & Thornhill, R. (1998). Bilateral symmetry and sexual selection: A meta-analysis. *The American Naturalist, 151*(2), 174–192. doi: 10.1086/286110

Morris, D. (1969). *The human zoo*. New York: McGraw-Hill.

Mueller, U., & Mazur, A. (1996). Facial dominance of West Point cadets as a predictor of later rank. *Social Forces, 74*, 823–850.

NHS :: The Nurses' Health Study. (n.d.). *Welcome to the Channing Laboratory Website*. Retrieved June 8, 2010, from http://www.channing.harvard.edu/nhs/

Paffenbarger, Jr., R. S., Blair, S. N., & Lee, I. (2001). A history of physical activity, cardiovascular health, and longevity: the scientific contributions of Jeremy N. Morris, DSc, DPH, FRCP. *International Journal of Epidemiology, 30*(5), 1184–1192.

Payne, B., Winakor, G., & Farrell-Beck, J. (1992). *The history of costume: From ancient Mesopotamia through the twentieth century.* New York: HarperCollins.

Ratey, J. J., & Hagerman, E. (2008). *Spark: The revolutionary new science of exercise and the brain.* New York: Little, Brown.

Report of the Dietary Guidelines Advisory Committee on Dietary Guidelines for Americans, 2005. (n.d.). *Health.gov | Your Portal to Health Information from the U.S. Government.* Retrieved June 1, 2010, from http://www.health.gov/dietaryguidelines/dga2005/report/

Singh, D. (1993). Adoptive significance of female physical attractiveness: role of waist to hip ratio. *Journal of Personality & Social Psychology, 65,* 293–307.

Smith, V. (2007). *Clean: A history of personal hygiene and purity.* Oxford, England: Oxford University Press.

Thornhill, R., & Gangestad, S. W. (1994). Human fluctuating asymmetry and sexual behavior. *Psychological Science, 5*(5), 297–302. doi: 10.1111/j.1467-9280.1994.tb00629.x

Townsend, J. M., & Levy, G. D. (1990). Effects of potential partners' physical attractiveness and socioeconomic status on sexuality and partner selection. *Archives of Sexual Behavior, 19*(2), 149–164. doi: 10.1007/BF01542229

Veblen, T. (1912). *The theory of the leisure class.* New York: MacMillan.

Wedekind, C., & Furi, S. (1997). Body odour preferences in men and women: Do they aim for specific MHC combinations or simply heterozygosity? *Proceedings of the Royal Society of London, Biological Sciences, 264*(1387), 1471–1479.

Chapter 3

Intellectuality Dimension

Intellectuality is the ability to have knowledge, to reason, and to understand. It is housed in our brain primarily, and requires electrical and chemical firing of neurons to function. This is similar to the hard drive in a computer—if it malfunctions intellectually, it can be affected.

Intellectuality also requires learning from the external environment, and it is stored on the neurons. Once this external learning begins, it becomes hardwired in the brain, through repetition, into memory. The memory that is formed is analogous to the software on a computer.

An aspect of human intellectuality that is unlike the above computer analogy is *thinking*. Computers do not literally think. They store information in the form of memory, but in human beings, the information is not only stored, it becomes integrated to various parts of the brain, which receives constant external stimulation from the environment. The interaction between the human brain's stored information and the constant stimulation from the environment enables it to ideate, which is the ability to create ideas (think outside the box) that enable humans to alter their environment and their reality. The ability to ideate is the key to thinking.

Intellectuality can therefore be summarized as the ability to store both knowledge and skills, and create new knowledge and skills via ideas to improve human existence.

Following are some facts regarding intellectuality.

Fact 1: Intellectuality is more than IQ scores on an intelligence test.

Many people believe that IQ scores reflect intellectuality. They do and they do not. They do in that they measure abilities necessary for intellectuality such as language skills, mathematical skills, abstract reasoning/problem solving, and knowledge storage ability.

Intellectuality is more than one's IQ scores, and so in many ways, IQ scores do not accurately reflect intellectuality. There are many people who have high IQ scores but cannot function in daily life well. In Wagner's essay "Why Smart People Do Dumb Things," Wagner points out that IQ tests measure what is known. They do not measure a person's ability to think beyond the known. They require a form of linear logic to be successful on them (Wagner, 2003).

Conversely, Wagner points out that real life has a lot of unknowns that require dynamic logic to survive (Wagner, 2003). IQ tests measure static intellectuality but not adaptive intellectuality. Human functioning requires constant adjustment intellectually.

In 1983, Howard Gardner published a book called *Frames of Mind*. It was not well-received by the intelligence testing community. Gardner basically stated that IQ tests do measure aspects of intelligence that are relevant to human functioning, but he hypothesized that there may be other forms of intelligence necessary for human functioning and success. He added five more types: bodily-kinesthetic (body movement, i.e., athleticism), musical (auditory intelligence), interpersonal (social), intrapersonal (emotional and self-knowledge), and existential (philosophical/moral) (Gardner, 1983). Gardner has gained more credibility since these initial ideas were introduced by publishing several books. The current criticism is there is very little testing and research to validate his work.

In Stephen Jay Gould's classic book *The Mismeasure of Man*, the author takes great issue with the fact that intelligence tests can be meaningful by determining the ranking of all people using a single number on what he calls a linear scale of intrinsic and unchangeable mental worth. Basically Gould believes that intelligence testing utilizes narrow and one-dimensional ways of measuring what intelligence is. Gould adds that this narrow approach creates a major philosophical error because it negates the social impact of nature, nurture, and genetics as factors affecting human functioning (Gould, 2008).

A third challenge to the issue of intellectuality and IQ testing is advocated by Robert Sternberg. Sternberg coined the term *successful intelligence,* which is broader than general intelligence as defined by IQ tests. Successful intelligence is defined as the "ability to achieve success in life in terms of one's personal standards within their socio-cultural context" (Sternberg, 1997). For example, if you achieve great success as a building contractor with only a high school degree, the measure of your intelligence is not your educational attainment. Your intelligence should be based on your success as a building contractor.

Sternberg defines successful intelligence as analytic ability, creative ability, and practical ability. The "analytic" ability is used to solve the problems. The "creative" ability is used to decide what problems to solve, and the "practical" ability is used to make solutions to a problem effective (Sternberg, 1997). Sternberg has been criticized by the intelligence testing community as not having sufficient science to support his theories. This is a legitimate observation, but Sternberg certainly poses food for thought.

The idea that achieving an "elite" IQ score on an intelligence test will result in an elite occupation or high social status later in life was challenged by an unlikely source, Lewis Terman. Terman, while a Stanford University professor, developed one of the first widely used intelligence tests, the Stanford-Binet.

One of Terman's major research efforts was the tracking of 1,470 children whose IQ averaged over 140 and ranged as high as 200. Some of these students were in the 99th percentile of the 99th percentile. This group of young geniuses came to be known as Terman's "Termites." Terman tracked this select group of students his whole career, believing their "genius" status would make them the future elite of the United States (Terman, Oden, & Bayley, 1947).

When the Termites reached adulthood, however, Terman's belief that high IQ determines the social elite was disproven. Although some of the Termite students achieved relative success, few were nationally known figures. Many earned relatively good incomes, but the majority ended up in careers that would be considered average, and many held jobs that Terman would have considered failures (Terman, Oden, & Bayley, 1947).

Fact 2: Memory is the foundation for intellectuality.

Memory is the critical factor in all learning. Without it, you would have significant problems not only intellectually but in day-to-day functioning. Many of the diseases of aging that are now plaguing us are memory disorders such as dementia and Alzheimer's. The greater our memory loss, the less able we are to function day-to-day.

Memory is very complicated. For example, there are different types of memory. There is short-term memory, which is the ability to remember something you just experienced such as a person's name or statement. There is long-term memory, which stores knowledge and skills for daily functioning. "Motor" memory is your body's ability to remember how to do something like riding a bicycle, and "episode" memory is a recall of events that take place in your life. There is "semantic" memory, which helps you remember words and their meaning. There are "sensory" memories, which involve "visual" (what was seen); "auditory" (what was heard); "olfactory" (what was smelled); "savory" (what was tasted); and "tactile" (what was touched).

In Daniel Schacter's book *The Seven Sins of Memory*, the author says there are seven factors that cause memory errors. The first is **transience,** which is memory loss due to the passage of time. We experience this every day when suddenly someone says something or something you read or see triggers a memory of the past (Schacter, 2002).

The second is **absent mindedness,** which is forgetting something that occurred because you were not paying attention while the event was occurring (Schacter, 2002). The classic example is when you lay down a set of keys or your wallet and did not pay attention while placing it. You then start looking for it, thinking you lost it, when in reality you just misplaced it.

The third is **blocking.** This occurs when you know you know but have forgotten (Schacter, 2002). The most common type of blocking is when you know a person's face and know what he or she does but cannot think of his or her name.

The fourth is **misattribution.** This occurs when pieces of memory are misconnected. This happens, for example, when you experience what some people call *déjà vu* (Schacter, 2002). You begin to believe you experienced something in the present that actually happened in the past. The reality is there are triggers in the present circumstances such as smells, sounds, or sights that actually occurred in a prior event. You inappropriately connect them to the present event because there are some similarities.

The fifth is **suggestibility.** This occurs when people incorporate misleading information from outside sources such as people, pictures, or the media into their personal recollection (Schacter, 2002). The most common happens in interviews of small children who may have been sexually abused. If the interviewer starts to suggest things to the child that might have occurred, but in truth did not, the child may actually say they did occur.

The sixth is **bias**. This occurs when your present memories are influenced by your own personal beliefs, feelings, and experiences from the past (Schacter, 2002). An example would be cultural or racial bias influencing your recall of a recent experience with someone from that race or culture. If you are negatively biased to begin with, you will impose those negative feelings/beliefs on your current recall experience even when they are inaccurate.

The last is **persistence.** This occurs when someone cannot let go of a memory and it affects their perception and feelings in the present (Schacter, 2002). The most common example would be post traumatic stress disorder, which is experienced by combat veterans, crime victims, and victims of other traumatic experiences. Their experiences are deeply imprinted in their memories.

Fact 3: There are various thinking disorders besides memory disorders that affect intellectuality.

Autistic savant is a term that describes people with uncanny intellectual abilities coupled with intellectual inabilities. *Savant* refers to being learned. *Autistic* refers to being self-absorbed and not aware of the outside world.

Kim Peek is probably the most well-known autistic savant. He was the basis for the movie *Rain Man* with Dustin Hoffman and Tom Cruise. Kim

Peek began reading at 18 months of age with no parental prompting. He was innately fascinated with words and obviously books.

Peek's ability to recall and absorb into memory what he had read was uncanny. He read thousands of books and was able to retain virtually everything he read in his permanent memory.

Despite this incredible ability, Peek had several intellectual disabilities. He was dependant on his father for his day-to-day functioning. He had difficulty socializing with people and had difficulty coping with a lack of structure. In general, Peek was comfortable with linear thinking (orderly) and uncomfortable with dynamic thinking.

People like Peek and their intellectual abilities and disabilities are expanding the boundaries of how to define thinking.

Fact 4: Intellectuality requires an ability to be thinking beyond what is directly seen or heard.

Psychologists use a term called *cognition*. Cognition is an ability to be aware. Being aware requires not only the storage of known knowledge and skills; it requires being aware of what is going beyond a conscious level.

Humans have five senses. They have eyes to see, ears to hear, a nose to smell, a mouth to taste, and skin to touch. These five senses are active at both a conscious level and an unconscious level, which is sometimes called intuition or unconscious intelligence.

For instance, bacteria in water cannot be seen by the naked eye. Before microscopes existed, humans became ill due to harmful bacteria in water. People knew they needed water to survive, but what they could not see was that certain bacteria were in the water. These harmful bacteria existed at an unconscious level until microscopes helped us see beyond the eye's natural ability. The microscope enables humans to actually see (be more aware) as to the direct cause of water-borne diseases.

Intellectuality requires awareness, but intellectuality also causes awareness. Our ancestors observed that water was keeping us alive and yet killing us at the same time. The question of why was considered over and over. Eventually this led to the idea that it was not water itself but something in some water that caused illness and death.

Fact 5: Intellectuality benefits from taking action on what you think.

One of the issues that is debated about regarding intelligence is the concept *book smart* versus *experience.* The book smart view is that people who have a lot of knowledge due to reading books and other sources of written information are often described as not being in touch with reality. The experience view advocates that the best teacher is action rather than words, but action by itself may not give rise to more knowledge.

Both perspectives have merit, but the combination of the two is probably the best approach in improving one's intellectuality. The danger of knowledge through words alone is that you might see the overall picture, but you lack the details that experience only can teach. Conversely, experience only creates the dilemma of "not seeing the forest for the trees." You are so enmeshed in the trees you cannot see the big picture.

In John Ratey's book *A User's Guide to the Brain*, Ratey discusses the concept of "motoring." Motoring refers to knowledge or insight the brain possesses being acted upon, which in turn expands and interprets that knowledge (Ratey, 2001). Reading a book on how to play golf, for example, is not as well understood by the brain unless it is acted upon. You have to swing the club based on the brain's knowledge from reading the book. Motoring solidifies learning primarily due to more neurons being dedicated to learning if the body and mind are simultaneously engaged. You tend to remember things you do rather than just think about.

Fact 6: Novelty can increase Intellectuality.

The tendency for humans to get comfortable with what is familiar presents problems for intellectuality. Whenever you have to think or act in a way that opposes how you already think or act, the brain and body resist. Their resistance is heightened if the habits you have are really ingrained.

For example, if you were to pick up a pen or pencil and write something using your opposing hand, you would resist. Your fingers would cramp up and your brain would tell you to stop. In reality, everyone can write with their opposing hand with practice, but at a young age, you began to write with one hand or the other. Although genetics can affect which way you choose to write, you can oppose your genetics of right-handedness or left-handedness if you choose to.

Intellectuality begins to expand if you force yourself to think and act in ways that are novel or new. This is a result of new neurons in the brain being activated for new learning to be acquired. When new neurons become engaged to new inputs, intellectual flexibility increases. The more flexible the brain becomes, the more accepting it is of new information. The benefits for intellectuality are greater because a person does not become set in his or her ways due to the brain's flexibility training. As one gets older, novelty could become difficult to achieve due to power of mental habits already ingrained due to aging.

Fact 7: Don't believe everything you think.

In Thomas Kida's *Don't Believe Everything You Think*, he discusses what he calls the six basic mistakes in thinking (2006). They are listed below:

1. We prefer stories over statistics.

It is in our nature as human beings to tell stories. Consequently, much of our learning about life is through storytelling or personal accounts about life. We are social animals, and we are very interested in other people's stories and how their experiences relate to us.

Unfortunately, generalizing about another person's life experience and connecting it to our own may not always be wise. Reading about another person's marriage or another person's success as a leader may help but may also hurt. We are unique individuals with unique circumstances given our genetics, prior experiences, biology, and learning, and assuming another person's perspective may not be wise, particularly since other people's stories often leave out or misinterpret facts that could be important in determining a good or bad outcome.

Statistics are dry and inanimate. They have no life to them and perhaps that is why many of us are not attracted to them. For example, your friend tells you a story about how great his make of automobile is and that, of course, you should purchase one like it. The statistics regarding the car's reliability and potential problems do not support your friend's anecdotal "evidence." Even though the statistics should have greater weight than the friend's advice, many give more credence to the anecdote.

2. We seek to confirm, not to question, our ideas.

It is in our nature to seek evidence or facts about what we think is true. If you believe that your friend who has been arrested for a serious crime or moral transgression cannot be guilty, you probably will not listen to facts that tell you otherwise. It is in our nature to avoid the anguish that conflicting facts can cause.

3. We rarely appreciate the role of chance and coincidence in shaping events.

We generally do not appreciate the fact that chance or coincidence plays a significant role in our lives. We want things to happen for a reason or believe it must have been fate.

It is ingrained in us to find cause and effect in things that happen to us. We therefore may assume we must have contracted a disease due to something we did wrong. We assume that we won two consecutive pots of money on a Las Vegas slot machine because it is our "lucky" day.

The reality is many things happen due to unknown causes or chance in terms of good and bad occurrences.

4. We sometimes misperceive the world around us.

Our perceptions about reality are frequently wrong. This is because our perceptions are greatly influenced by faulty or minimal exposure to facts or experiences related to realities we are not familiar with. They are also influenced by what we expect to see or want to see.

A lack of experience or viable facts regarding a religion or culture can conjure some unwarranted prejudices. If you were to watch television in America and notice that terrorists committing violent acts were believers in the Islamic religion you might perceive that Islamic religion, professes violence. It does not. If you watch movies regarding World War II and Nazi Germany, you might perceive that the German soldiers were all Nazis. The fact is, there were well over 100 documented attempts on Hitler's life by German officers.

5. We tend to oversimplify our thinking.

There is no doubt that the amount of information available to us today is overwhelming. This can cause what is sometimes referred to as analysis paralysis, and therefore, there is a need to simplify. This simplification process can often lead us to select information that is easily accessible and ignore information that is more relevant.

For instance you read in the newspaper about a scientific study that a certain pain medication on the market has been associated with an increase in heart attacks. You immediately quit using the medication even though you have been using it for six months, experiencing neither pain nor side effects.

The pain medication study results showed that 5 people in a placebo group who were not taking the medication had heart attacks. In addition, 10 people in the treatment group who were taking the pain medication had heart attacks. The study concludes there was 100 percent greater chance of heart attack for those taking the medication. The statement is true based on the numbers, but is it?

A closer reading of the study yields that this was the first study tracking the new medication. There were 400 people in the treatment group taking the medication in which 10 had heart attacks. The size of the placebo group not taking the medication was 300.

The question becomes that a greater examination of the information in the study should make you question the results for the following reason. The first reason is that of the 400 who took the medication, only 10 had heart attacks. Based on that information, there is only a 2.5 percent chance of a heart attack for people who take the medication.

The second reason the results need to be reconsidered is that 390 people out of 400 did not have a heart attack and received pain relief. The relief of pain may be worth the 2.5 percent risk.

A third reason is the results are from one study where the sample groups used to measure were of unequal size; 400 receiving the medication and 300 not receiving. Group size in treatment versus control research should be as equal as possible. It could be that adding another 100 people to the placebo group could result in 2 more people having heart attacks, which would mean 7 had heart attacks with no pain medication versus 10 with. This means there is a 2.3 percent chance of heart attack by not taking the medication and 2.5 percent chance of heart attack by taking the medication.

6. We have faulty memories.

Human memories are not very good in terms of accurate recall or recall in general. Research has shown (mentioned earlier) that our memories can change. You are capable of creating new memories for events that never happened. You can exaggerate to the positive or negative the facts of prior events due to emotions or ego. You can change memories due to expectations, the environment, or even suggestive questions from others.

All of the mistakes mentioned above are excellent reasons for not trusting your thinking and should be considered before one acts on what they think.

Humans often confuse their thinking as being reality or truth. The best way to avoid faulty thinking is to consider Kida's six reasons. It also helps to gather pertinent facts that can validate what you think.

For example, these steps would be helpful in purchasing an automobile, deciding a health issue, or choosing how to get to a location. There are sources that have facts to support or disprove what you think. In purchasing an automobile, consider an unbiased source such as *Consumer Reports*; do not buy it just because you like it. In deciding how to proceed with a health issue, get a second and even a third opinion from unbiased sources, not hearsay from a friend. In travel directions, consider both maps and GPS systems, not your own sense of direction.

Fact 8: Facts are not necessarily truth.

Facts and intellectuality are intertwined. Facts are defined as things that are known to have occurred, to exist, or to be true. The storing of facts is critical to intellectuality because facts are used to determine not only what could be true but possible courses of actions based on the facts.

Unfortunately, even "facts" are not always reliable for many reasons. The first reason is facts may be true in a moment in time but not necessarily applicable to a future event or to other facts. For example, it may be a fact that a person who you are trying to hire for a job received great recommendations from several references. The assumption may be that these past positive references reflect present or future behavior in that person. The problem is human behavior is often transient. How a person may have acted in the past may not occur in the present or future. This is because the potential employee may have personal problems outside the job while working for you that causes them to behave in ways that do not match prior behavior.

A person's behavior is also influenced by context. A nonviolent person may become violent due to situational variables that trigger the violence. It is possible these triggers were unknown to the nonviolent person until they occurred.

Facts can also be faulty based on quality of the sources that dispense the facts. Let's take the example of the person mentioned above who comes highly recommended for a job. It is possible that the quality of the information may in fact be inaccurate for several possible reasons. Maybe the reference is leaving out negative facts about this person because he or she is trying to get rid of this person. Maybe the reference is a personal friend of the person and is trying to protect the person's negative qualities from being known. Maybe the reference has been told that what he or she says about the person is accessible to the person. The reference therefore does not want to cause problems if he or she says something negative about the person. It is therefore obvious why humans' hearsay about facts can be unreliable.

The way to respond to the above situation is to rely on facts that supposedly remove the human element. This is sometimes defined as scientific facts. There is an assumption that if a fact is scientific, it is irrefutable. For example, DNA is now used as irrefutable evidence in many criminal cases. Many people assume that DNA is absolute truth or fact. There is no doubt that using DNA results is significantly better than letting human opinion such as eyewitness facts determine guilt or innocence.

Unfortunately, DNA has the potential for error due to a phenomenon called *cell fusion.* Cell fusion refers to the possibility that another person's cells could be in your body for a variety of reasons, and this could affect DNA. Cell fusion can be caused by blood transfusions or organ transplants. And while scientists will admit that this is possible, they minimize it. When scientists are asked how minimal (in statistical numbers), they say they cannot answer that. It is also important to keep in mind that DNA information is managed by humans and reported by humans. Humans have been known to make mistakes.

Facts may represent partial truth but not the whole truth. The John Grisham book *The Innocent Man* (2006) is based on an actual case of two men, Ron Williamson and Dennis Fritz, who were convicted of murdering a waitress from a restaurant they patronized the night before she was murdered. The facts that drove this case were they were seen talking with her in the restaurant, one of the defendants had a prior criminal record, hair fiber evidence of the men were found at the crime scene and the victim's apartment, and a witness in the restaurant reported that the waitress told him she was uncomfortable with the two men. Williamson and Fritz were subsequently convicted with one receiving the death penalty and the other a life sentence in prison.

After several attempts by Williamson to get his death sentence reversed, he finally found an attorney to take the case. The attorney asked for DNA evidence in the case. The DNA did not match the death row inmate's DNA. The DNA evidence did match a known sex offender serving time in a prison in another state. The sex offender was the witness in the restaurant who told investigators the two men were bothering the waitress. He obviously lied to send the investigators in a different direction.

The hair evidence at the crime scene was likely there because some of the defendant's hair fibers evidently got on the waitress's clothing the night before in the restaurant. The hair stuck to her clothing which hair will do, and the hairs were carried to the crime scene by the victim.

Facts by themselves may either not reflect the whole truth or they may not be quality facts.

Fact 9: Linear thinking versus dynamic thinking depends on the situation.

Linear thinking assumes there is order to reality, which there is in many instances. *Linear* is derived from the word *line,* as in straight line. Linear thinking, applied to day-to-day reality, assumes that determining the progression of facts in a situation leads to a better outcome. Linear thinking also implies that doing things in a step-by-step fashion produces the better outcome.

Linear thinking is best applied to managing inanimate objects—things that are not alive. For example, in building trades, linear thinking is critical to success. Carpenters, plumbers, and electricians must apply a systematic (linear) thinking to ensure the proper installation of the wood structure, the plumbing pipes, and electrical wiring.

Dynamic thinking involves adaptive/changing logic to situations. In dynamic thinking, there may not be a proven step-by-step (linear) approach to solving a problem. Life has many constantly changing and unpredictable circumstances where there are no established facts that support a certain way of doing things.

Laws created by humans to control how society runs are an attempt to apply linear thinking to a dynamic reality. This linear thinking can be successful in many instances but also unsuccessful in many instances when the rule of law is universally applied. When this happens, the term *common sense* arises.

Common sense is an attempt to apply dynamic logic to a situation to which linear logic does not apply. For instance, law enforcement officers find themselves in many situations that applying the rule of law is not logical or does not make sense. Law enforcement will make them apply dynamic logic. This is often called officer discretion. The facts in the case may warrant applying the rule of law (linear), but doing so would cause more harm and lead to an unsuccessful outcome.

For example, an officer sees a young teenager driving by, and the teen appears to be driving above the speed limit. The officer immediately does a U-turn but decides to drive slowly behind the speeding teenager. The teenager starts to speed up even further upon seeing the officer. The officer realizes that the teenage driver will be coming up on a school zone area in about two miles at about the time school is letting out. The officer takes down the tag number and breaks off following the teenage driver. The officer does a right turn as if he is not pursuing the speeding vehicle anymore.

In the above instance, the officer had legal grounds (linear logic) to pursue the speeding teenager, but he used discretion. The officer's common sense (dynamic logic) told him that a high speed chase near a school zone could do more harm than good. He did take down the tag number of the vehicle to do a follow-up visit to the owner of the vehicle later on in the day.

Fact 10: We use both conscious intelligence and unconscious intelligence, depending on the situation.

In Malcolm Gladwell's best selling book *Blink* (2005), Gladwell discusses thinking that is done with analytical precision that could be described as *conscious intelligence* and thinking that is done in the blink of an eye called *unconscious intelligence.* Gladwell gives examples of both types of intelligences or thinking that have successful outcomes. He also points out the dangers of both causing unsuccessful outcomes.

An example of unconscious intelligence being successful is the Iowa Card Players Experiment discussed in Gladwell's book. In this study, there are two sets of players: one group of nonprofessional card players and the other professional card players. The two groups are given two sets of cards—a blue deck and a red deck. The cards contain sums of money printed on the non-face side. The players are to turn over the cards one-by-one from either deck randomly.

The red deck of cards contains large sums of money printed on them that can be lost or won. The players can win a good profit if they use the blue deck of cards. If they continue to use the red deck, they will lose money. After 8 to 10 moves, the professional players begin to feel uneasiness (unconscious intelligence) with the red deck, but after 30 moves, they realize that by leaving the red deck alone, they will win. The nonprofessional players do not experience uneasiness until the 30th to 40th card, but then realize after 80 card moves that sticking with the blue deck is the best bet.

It appears that the professional players' unconscious intelligence kicked in more rapidly than the nonprofessional players, probably due to experience. The professional players' conscious intelligence also kicked in more rapidly than the nonprofessional players. Unconscious intelligence is often synonymous with terms like *intuition, ESP,* or *gut feeling.*

An example of the criticality of the unconscious becoming conscious intelligence at work is John Gottman's research on marital success (2005). Gottman, who teaches and conducts much of his research at the University of Washington, is able to predict divorce in a married couple within 15 years by observing the couple talk about a relationship problem for 15 minutes. The system is called *Specific Affect (SAAFF) Coding System.*

The SAAFF Coding System involves videotaping couples and measuring the various emotions they communicate in facial expression and voice intonation. The emotions are measured in one-second clips. In a 15-minute dialogue, each couple has communicated 900 one-second voice tones and facial displays. By analyzing these one-second clips that reflect what is going on below the conscious level of the couples, Gottman sees emotional patterns that predict success or failure in a long-term relationship.

Gottman has found that constant facial and vocal displays of four emotions, *disgust*, *contempt*, *stonewalling* and *belligerence,* are the critical emotions that predict divorce long term.

Gottman also advocates, based on this analysis of couples, that for every negative emotion conveyed by a couple, five positive emotions are necessary for the relationship to thrive. If the five positive to one negative emotion ratio starts to regress, the couple's chances for relationship success becomes less over time.

Gottman research demonstrates the need to bring unseen/unknown facts to a conscious level so that we can correct problems.

Developing and Applying Your Intellectuality

Factual Ability

> "The frontiers are not east or west, north or south, but wherever a man fronts a fact."
>
> – Henry David Thoreau

The danger of using facts to describe truth was discussed earlier in this chapter. Facts were defined as things that are known to have been observed or to be true.

The first step in looking at facts is determining the quality of the facts. Quality of facts is determined by sources. The first level of factual quality, and probably the weakest, is when the fact comes from another person. This is when someone reports a fact based on what they heard or observed. For example, someone says to you that they overheard a conversation at a restaurant yesterday that John Smith is leaving his wife.

The problem with the above should be obvious. First of all this source of data is called *gossip* in some instances. It is not that fact is untrue—it could be true. The problem is these sources of facts are often questionable due to a lack of substantiation called *hearsay*. It could be your friend overheard it from someone else who heard it from another party. The problem with hearsay is that facts often get embellished and off-track due to human beings' inability to listen well or their tendency to misconstrue what they hear or see.

The second level of factual quality is the expertise of the person who is communicating the facts. For example, someone who is reporting medical advice to another and is not a physician should be a red flag to the listener regarding factual quality. Human beings have an unfortunate tendency to assume expertise in subjects in which they are not educated.

The third level of factual quality is a supposed nonhuman source. A nonhuman source is one in which the facts communicator read about the fact. There is the assumption that the written word makes a fact a fact. In other words, it must be true if it is written about. The problem here is the written word is from a human source called the writer. There are often checks and balances on a writer's reporting of the facts. Writers are often asked to substantiate their sources for what they write about. This can help but does not guarantee the quality of facts, especially when their sources are other people.

The fourth level of factual quality is when the individual human bias source is removed as much as possible. It is often referred to as a form of scientific research where several people taking a survey are asked for their opinion about something. The premise here is that the more minds (i.e., people) involved in determining the facts, the better the chances of truth.

The obvious example of this is a political election or a product survey. Unfortunately, despite the superiority of more minds being better than one, the problem of fact validity is still a problem. There is an assumption that a group of people has sufficient expertise on a subject. This is sometimes resolved by putting together a panel of experts versus one expert to debate the facts.

The fifth level of factual quality is the highest level of scientific research. It employs what is called the *scientific method*. The scientific method starts out with a hypothesis. The hypothesis is a theory, idea, or perception about a possible fact.

An example of a hypothesis could be "aerobic exercise decreases heart disease." The scientific method then sets out to prove whether this is true, untrue, or somewhat true through controlled experimentation. The controlled experimentation is an attempt to remove human bias altogether and utilizes a treatment versus a controlled approach. The treatment approach would be having a group of people perform aerobic exercise over time and see if it shows positive effects on heart functioning such as blood pressure. The controlled approach would be to have a group not do aerobic exercise over time and see its effect on blood pressure.

There are two problems with the above approach in determining fact. One, it may be that the one experiment showed positive results, but that could be unique to the two groups tested or other factors not controlled for. This problem is resolved by what scientists call replication of the research. By replicating the research several times and still getting the same outcome, truth is more likely true.

The second problem is the issue of error variance. Error variance means there may have been variables unaccounted for other than exercise that caused improved heart health. One type is called the placebo/halo effect. It could be those people in the experiment believed the exercise was helping and therefore it helped. How much did their belief in mind over matter contribute to a positive outcome?

It is obvious at this point that factual quality is not easy to achieve even when rigorous science tries to prove it. It is also difficult when a decision about truth does not allow for time and time is crucial. Despite this, it is important not to act on facts that are not valid because doing so can be harmful.

A person who has exemplified this dimension is Francis S. Collins.

Francis S. Collins, M.D.—Director, National Institute for Health

Francis S. Collins, M.D., is the current National Institutes of Health Director and former Director of the Human Genome Project. He has supervised thousands of scientists from around the world over several years to bring together the facts regarding human genome. He also bridged the gap with Craig Venter, the private entrepreneur, by insuring the public access to that data.

Even though Francis Collins initially saw himself pursuing chemistry rather than biology, he happened to take a biochemistry course that led him to the study of DNA and RNA. Collins finished his doctoral program in physical chemistry and then entered medical school and began studying medical genetics. After completing prestigious fellowships and internships, he landed at the University of Michigan where he began crossing DNA strands to identify abnormal genes. This helped him isolate the genes that caused various disorders.

Beginning with the identification of the genes responsible for cystic fibrosis and ultimately Huntington's, which Collins said was "the longest and most

---

(continued)

frustrating search in the annals of molecular biology," Collins decided to pursue a very grand idea.

Collins and his group of researchers wanted next to pursue mapping the entire human genome. By 2003, the mapping was complete, far ahead of schedule. As Collins, et al. have proceeded with their research, their fact-finding mission to discover the functions of all genes gives hope to the idea that ultimately all mysterious diseases can be fought against effectively. *"What more powerful form of study of mankind could there be than to read our own instruction book?"* Collins said ("Francis Collins Interview—Academy of Achievement," 2010).

Conceptual Ability

Conceptualizing is the ability to generate ideas or hypothesize about how to explain life phenomena and address problems that affect life. It is an ability to think outside what is known. It involves developing theories of why certain things occur in life. It is sometimes referred to as abstract reasoning. An abstraction is defined as a product of human imagination. The key word is *imagination.* Imagination is the ability to form ideas about things that exist beyond the human senses. In other words, just because something cannot be seen or heard does not mean it does not or cannot exist.

Albert Einstein's theory of relativity is considered by most scientists to be the critical theory that changed the science of physics. Alexander Graham Bell's theories created the telephone. Thomas Edison's theories created the application of electricity to everyday life. You cannot see relativity (atomic particles) directly with the naked eye. You cannot see words being transmitted through a telephone line. You cannot see electricity directly running through the electrical line (although you can see a spark from electricity). All of the these are examples of conceptualizing because they cannot be seen directly with the naked eye, but they do exist.

Many concepts or ideas are faulty because they have not been proven to exist. Many ideas or concepts have caused harm because they were not fully researched before they were applied.

72

For example, it was theorized during the Middle Ages that disease in the body was carried through the blood stream. That is true. The problem was it was also theorized if blood was drained from an affected person, the disease would be drained away as well. This medical approach was called blood letting. Unfortunately, if too much blood was drained from people, they died.

The ability to conceptualize is probably innate as well as nurtured. It involves several abilities that are discussed below.

The first is to trust/believe that what is not directly available to the senses (eyes, ears, nose, taste, and smell) may still exist. There is a tendency for some humans to assume it is not real if it cannot be sensed. The typical comments from people who operate this way are "you need to get in touch with reality," "common sense tells you that if you cannot see it, it doesn't exist," or "I don't believe in things I can't see, touch, or smell."

It is important to note that it would be naïve to act upon a theory that is unproven. Many people have lost their lives placing faith in faulty ideas, beliefs, or theories. For example, there are some who believe that a child with a serious documented medical problem can be cured by prayer when there is clear evidence that the child will die from the illness without medical interventions.

Conversely, conceptualizing about the cause of a disease and then a possible cure is a worthy endeavor. For example, in Francis Collins's book *The Language of God* (2006) mentioned earlier, Collins (the leading scientist in the Human Genome Project) discusses how difficult it was to prove and determine what gene causes cystic fibrosis in children. Collins reported that it took 2,000 scientists 10 years at a cost of $50 million to do this. Collins is a Christian and yet a noted scientist who realizes the value of both belief (conceptualizing) and science (proving beyond the senses).

Another critical factor in conceptualizing is the appreciation of dynamic thinking as well as linear thinking. Dynamic thinking realizes that not all awareness of our world is predictable, known, and unchangeable. IQ tests measure known, predictable, and changeable language ability, mathematical ability, spatial ability, and certain types of memory. These abilities are critical to human development and growth. They are necessary, but are they sufficient?

In Howard Gardner's book *Multiple Intelligence* published in 1983, Gardner discussed the possibility/theory that there are other forms of intelligence that exist, that need to be measured, and that should be valued in human functioning. These were Bodily-Kinesthetic (athletic), Auditory (musical), Interpersonal (social), Intrapersonal (emotional), and Existential (philosophical). Gardner's book was not well accepted at that time by traditional thinkers on intelligence. Today, despite his popularity, and his many converts who believe that there are more forms of intelligence than what IQ tests measure, there are still many detractors. Gardner demonstrated dynamic thinking when he strayed from traditional views of IQ and what intelligence may be.

Another ability in conceptualizing is a willingness to expose your mind to unfamiliar experiences and knowledge. Psychologists call this ability the *personality trait of openness* (DiSalvo, 2010). There is a tendency for many of us, especially with aging, to feel uncomfortable with the unfamiliar. Our bodies and minds like predictable, habitual experiences because they do not require much thinking.

One of the ways to test openness in yourself is to travel to a culture where you do not know the language or customs. If you cannot travel to a foreign land, allow yourself to be around people who normally make you uneasy due to their appearance, race, or status. A third way is to read a book that exposes a set of values or beliefs that personally trouble you.

A fourth ability in conceptualizing is to realize how little you know and will ever know about life and how to live it. All too often, people who are successful in certain aspects of life think they know everything. Just because you have earned a master's degree does not mean you will be successful as a parent or friend. Just because you can toss a football 70 yards for a touchdown does not mean you will be a success in managing your finances or personal relationships. Just because you are the leader in an organization does not mean you are smarter than the ones you lead.

It is difficult for certain people to admit they do not know as much as they think when they are good at doing certain things and receive praise for it. Unfortunately, these people can subsequently become blind to their own flaws, even when these flaws are seen by others. Confidence can make a person feel good. Self doubt makes people feel uneasy.

A possible solution to people's inability to accept how little they do know is to appreciate what they already know but to seek further knowledge as an adventure. In reality, the brain is often attracted to novelty or new knowledge. Once new knowledge is sought, it can become addictive. It is analogous to a world traveler's experiences, where every day can present new stimulation for the senses.

A person who has exemplified this dimension is Mario J. Molina.

Mario J. Molina, Ph.D.— Nobel Prize in Chemistry

Mario J. Molina, Ph.D., is a chemist who proved that the climate change in the ozone layer, etc., was being affected by environmental pollution and other factors. He did this despite political factions opposed to his view. He did this due to his persistence and his willingness to present the facts that supported his concepts.

When Molina presented his hypothesis in 1974 about the degree to which chlorofluorocarbons (CFCs) can harm (delete) the ozone layer, he was criticized and even ridiculed by CFC manufacturers as well as some of his fellow scientists.

Molina pressed on with his research, and in 1979, a National Academy of Sciences report confirmed Molina's premises. Finally, in 1985, the discovery of a large hole in the ozone layer over Antarctica authenticated Molina's hypothesis.

Although response was gradual, production of CFCs has virtually stopped. Molina continued his research and ultimately won the Nobel Prize for Chemistry in 1995. *"Finding out for myself, for the first time, how something works is really an enormous driving force,"* Molina said ("Mario Molina Biography—Academy of Achievement," 2010).

Logic Ability

> "Loyalty to a petrified opinion never yet broke a chain or freed a human soul."
>
> – Mark Twain

Logic is defined as the ability to reason or be rational. Synonyms for *logic* other than reason are *sound, cogent, coherent, well organized, clear, consistent,* and *relevant.*

Logic assumes that there is a systematic and developmental way to look at a problem. *Systematic* refers to the belief there is a common thread between events. *Developmental* means there is a step-by-step process to ensure accurate and efficient solutions to the problem.

For example, before going to a grocery store to purchase food, the first step would be to see what you need. A possible second step, if you want to have certain meals, is to write out a menu. Once the menu is written, you would need to determine what ingredients you do or do not have. A possible third step, if you collect coupons, is to gather the coupons that are relevant to your purchases. A fourth step is to write up a master list of what you are going to need. These steps are systematic and developmental. They force you to reason in a logical step-by-step manner before you act. Many people are not logical, and they just go to the store. By doing so they run the risk of being inaccurate (forget to purchase something they need) and inefficient (having to go back to the store—wasting time—to purchase something they forgot). A systematic, developmental approach is more logical because time and accuracy matter.

A second factor in logic is the ability to assemble all the information available that is relevant to a problem you are trying to solve or decision you are trying to make. The problem in these situations is having the relevant information to make an informed decision. A method for resolving this is to do research. With today's information resources (i.e., the Internet), research can be quick and efficient. The problem is the research information may not meet the accuracy criteria. This was discussed earlier in the chapter under factual skills. A decision or course of action is only as good as the quality of the facts that affect it.

When purchasing a new automobile, for example, there are information resources that are quite reliable and there are some that are not. The reliable ones are usually the ones that are promoting the product with no bias or benefit from promoting. A consumer magazine that recommends a certain automobile but also runs commercial ads for the automobile may not be a good information choice. A consumer magazine that does not use advertisements of any kind is probably a better choice.

There are decision-making situations where the information sources are not easily accessible. An example would be a medical decision. In this instance, most people will go along with one physician's recommendation. Unfortunately this may not be the most reliable source. One of the ways to address this is to seek a second opinion from another doctor with expertise in the problem or decision you are trying to make. If a third opinion were possible, that would be even better.

A good indicator of your own physician's information integrity is to ask him or her about a second opinion. If your doctor thinks it is a good idea and does not act defensively over the suggestion, it tells you a lot about your physician. It tells you that he or she feels confident in his or her diagnosis but has the ability to trust that he or she could be wrong. You also should consider doing your own research in a medical problem as well as consult various physicians.

The bottom line with getting good information before making a major decision is to assess the quality of the facts and the sources for those facts.

Another aspect of logic is to consider more than one course of action to solve a problem. This is best if time allows and the courses of action are known and reliable to you. In many instances, there is a tendency to think there is only one way to solve a problem. This is where the conceptualizing ability discussed above comes into play. When forced with a decision or a problem to solve, the more ideas generated to solve the problem, the greater chance of selecting the right one.

This can be a mentally and emotionally draining approach, but if a decision you make can affect your life significantly, it should be considered. For instance, the decision to leave a job, to go back to school, to get married, to start a business, or to have children are decisions that can have significant impact on you and possibly others. The quality of the information you bring to the decision making affects its success.

Let's say you have decided to start a business of your own. It involves a restaurant. Before seeking the money to start one, there are some critical facts to consider. The number one factor is the restaurant competition and how you measure up against it. The question is how do you get quality factual information on your competition? Asking your friends' opinions is probably not good enough. Riding around and looking at types of restaurants may or may not be sufficient. Surveying the demographics in the surrounding community to determine the number of people who might like your type of restaurant is a good place to start fact gathering. Visiting the various restaurants that might compete with you is another way to gather information, as is going to the local chamber of commerce for information on restaurants that have succeeded or failed in the market in which you are interested.

There can be a problem of what is sometimes called *analysis paralysis,* which is discussed in Malcolm Gladwell's book *Blink* (2005). Analysis paralysis occurs when too much information interferes with the accuracy of decision making. Often times, it is difficult to sort through an excess of information and find that which is truly critical to making a judgment. We think that collecting more and more information will help us make the best decision or reinforce a decision we have already made, when in fact it obfuscates the process and does not make the decision more accurate. Sometimes the information we collect is relevant to the situation at the time, but other unpredictable factors change the playing field.

In your decision to open a restaurant discussed above, it appears that all the initial factors to be considered did indeed impact the decision to start the restaurant. Unfortunately as you begin the process to open your restaurant, another restaurant with a similar menu *and* a chain restaurant with a lot of supportive capital, brand name recognition, and patent marketing decide to open restaurants in the same area. This information was not there when you decided to open your restaurant.

The way to manage the potential problem of analysis paralysis is to develop a change strategy that anticipates the unpredictable or unconsidered factors. This allows for a type of damage control to change a decision with minimal damage. It is like a fall-back position or retreat before too much damage is done. It causes minimal regret and maximum return.

A person who has exemplified this dimension is Anthony M. Kennedy.

Anthony M. Kennedy—Justice of the U.S. Supreme Court

Anthony M. Kennedy is the Supreme Court Justice whose nonpartisan interpretation of the law reflects this logical ability.

Kennedy has long had a reputation for fairness when it comes to deciding the cases before him. Before he was nominated and subsequently confirmed for a seat on the high court, his record in the U.S. Court of Appeals (9th Circuit) was largely conservative, but even then, he was known for his individualistic and practical approach to reviewing and deciding cases.

All in all, his decisions can be labeled neither conservative nor liberal; his leanings change based on the case at hand. In cases of criminal law, his interpretations tend to be conservative, but when it has come to cases of personal privacy, his interpretations have been more liberal.

Kennedy has justifiably earned a reputation for being temperate and objective. *"Our system presumes that there are certain principles that are more important than the temper of our times,"* Kennedy said ("Anthony Kennedy Biography—Academy of Achievement," 2005).

Operationalizing Ability

> "Ideas not coupled with actions never become bigger than the brain cells they occupy."
>
> – Arnold H. Glasgow

When you have logic to decide a course of action, you need to operationalize that action for success. Operationalizing is the ability to take a concept/idea that is supported by logically determined facts and put it into action in an organized way.

In building a house, there are pictures and blueprints that allow for visualization of what the house should look like and a set of blueprints that need to be put into action for the house to become a reality. The pictures and blueprints increase the builders' chance of a successful operationalization.

Now the building of the house begins but the operationalizing requires actions that are logical. In other words, the actions taken to build the house should be sequential for success. Below is an example of what those logical steps should be:

Step 1: Set the foundation
Step 2: Framing
Step 3: Sub-roof and sub-sizing
Step 4: Sub-flooring
Step 5: Shingling or covered sub-roofing
Step 6: Siding and windows
Step 7: Plumbing (pipes, sinks, tubs, etc.)
Step 8: Electricity (wiring and wiring boxes)
Step 9: Sheet rocking
Step 10: Trim work
Step 11: Driveway and walkways
Step 12: Hang doors and hardware
Step 13: Painting exterior and interior
Step 14: Flooring (carpet, tile, wood)
Step 15: Landscaping

The above sequencing is important because it increases the chances for the building of the house to be done efficiently and accurately.

Unfortunately when transitioning from logic to action, another phenomenon takes place. A form of dynamic logic occurs, which is the second aspect of operationalizing. This second phase is called *action logic.* Action logic is the ability to adapt to the linear plan of action that is running into problems.

Several factors can affect the orderly building of the house. Weather can be a big factor when a house is being built. Incompetent carpenters, roofers, electricians, or plumbers who can do something wrong can cause new problems. The materials used to build the house may be of poor quality or the incorrect size when they arrive to be used. These factors that were not planned for or expected require that those building the house change direction or deviate from their linear logic. They now have to adapt to the dynamic aspects of going from ideal to real. This is the real test of intellectualizing abilities.

In some instances, an experienced builder knows what to do right away. An inexperienced builder may not and hopefully realizes that. The inexperienced builder looks at the facts (the problems) and does not ignore them or do anything that might make the situation worse. This might involve covering up the problem by acting like it does not exist or rationalizing that wrong is right. In the wrong scenario, the inexperienced builder continues to use poor quality materials or hides problems behind walls (poor electrical or plumbing applications).

When running into unanticipated problems, the intellectuality techniques become the most difficult to apply. This requires individuals in these situations to have superior intellectual fitness, preventing inappropriate emotions, morality, or impulsive action from ruling the situation.

A person who has exemplified this dimension is Norman E. Borlaug.

Norman E. Borlaug, Ph.D.—The Father of the Green Revolution

Norman E. Borlaug, Ph.D., took his ideas on plant pathology and genetics and was able to operationalize his ideas around the world and therefore increase the planet's food supply.

The father of the "green revolution," Borlaug made incredible contributions to the development of high-yield crop varieties in the late 1940s and 1950s. Many experts agree that Borlaug's green revolution prevented large-scale global famine.

Borlaug began his work in Mexico where, with his mentor, he found that wheat crops were dying of disease. In addition to breeding disease-resistant seed, Borlaug also realized that crops could be raised during two seasons there. Mexico's food supply increased dramatically.

Even though he encountered resistance from native farmers at first, Borlaug took his seed and cultivation methods to Asia, and ultimately food production in Pakistan and India, for example, quadrupled.

Using a systematic approach, Borlaug transformed world food production. It is estimated that the green revolution saved one billion lives. *"The only way that the world can keep up with food production is by the improvement of science and technology,"* Borlaug said ("Norman Borlaug Biography—Academy of Achievement," 2009).

Intellectuality Test

Let's measure your intellectuality potential.

Below are some actions that measure your intellectuality skills. Rate the statements honestly. Use the following scale and place a check (✓) in the box to rate yourself for each statement.

1 = Rarely   2 = Sometimes   3 = Usually   4 = Often   5 = A Lot

You may want to ask some people who know you well to rate you, using the same scale. See how closely your score and their scores match. Don't be surprised if there is a big difference.

	1	2	3	4	5
1. You watch television shows that discuss scientific topics.	❏	❏	❏	❏	❏
2. You think the Internet can be an unreliable source of information.	❏	❏	❏	❏	❏
3. You read magazines like *Consumer Reports, Popular Mechanics,* and *Scientific American.*	❏	❏	❏	❏	❏
4. You like reading about various cultures.	❏	❏	❏	❏	❏
5. You like to experiment with new ideas by trying them out.	❏	❏	❏	❏	❏
6. When you are faced with a problem, you seek information regarding the problem from written sources such as books and research journals on that particular problem.	❏	❏	❏	❏	❏
7. You consider the reliability of sources from which you get your information.	❏	❏	❏	❏	❏
8. You write out on paper a list of things you need to do every day.	❏	❏	❏	❏	❏

	1	2	3	4	5
9. You write down ideas that come into your head so that you will not forget them.	❏	❏	❏	❏	❏
10. You lay out materials or tools necessary to complete a task before starting on it.	❏	❏	❏	❏	❏

Scoring:

Add your total score and multiply the total by 2. This number is your ability potential in this dimension. For example: $30 \times 2 = 60\%$ ability in this range.

A score above 80% is a good score.

A score above 90% is an excellent score.

Note: A more accurate assessment of your ability in this dimension, which consists of 40 statements/questions versus the 10 shown in this book, can be found at www.sotelligence.com.

References

Anthony Kennedy Biography—Academy of Achievement. (2005, September 4). *Academy of Achievement Main Menu*. Retrieved December 18, 2010, from http://www.achievement.org/autodoc/page/ken0bio-1

Collins, F. S. (2006). *The language of God: A scientist presents evidence for belief*. New York: Free Press.

DiSalvo, D. (2010). Are social networks messing with your head? *Scientific American Mind, 20*(7), 48–55.

Francis Collins Interview—Academy of Achievement. (2010, September 10). *Academy of Achievement Main Menu*. Retrieved December 17, 2010, from http://www.achievement.org/autodoc/page/col1int-1

Gardner, H. (1983). *Frames of mind: The theory of multiple intelligences*. New York: Basic Books.

Gladwell, M. (2005). *Blink: The power of thinking without thinking*. New York: Little, Brown and Company.

Gottman, J. M. (2005). *The mathematics of marriage: Dynamic nonlinear models*. Cambridge, MA: MIT Press.

Gould, S. J. (2008). *The mismeasure of man*. New York: W. W. Norton.

Grisham, J. (2006). *The innocent man: Murder and injustice in a small town*. New York: Doubleday.

Kida, T. E. (2006). *Don't believe everything you think: The 6 basic mistakes we make in thinking*. Amherst, NY: Prometheus Books.

Mario Molina Biography—Academy of Achievement. (2010, August 24). *Academy of Achievement Main Menu*. Retrieved December 17, 2010, from http://www.achievement.org/autodoc/page/mol0bio-1

Norman Borlaug Biography—Academy of Achievement. (2009, September 13). *Academy of Achievement Main Menu*. Retrieved December 18, 2010, from http://www.achievement.org/autodoc/page/bor0bio-1

Ratey, J. J. (2001). *A user's guide to the brain: Perception, attention, and the four theaters of the brain*. London: Little, Brown and Company.

Schacter, D. L. (2002). *The seven sins of memory: How the mind forgets and remembers*. Boston: Houghton Mifflin.

Sternberg, R. J. (1997). *Successful intelligence: How practical and creative intelligence determine success in life*. New York: Plume.

Terman, L. M., Oden, M. H., & Bayley, N. (1947). *The gifted child grows up: Twenty-five years' follow-up of a superior group*. Stanford, CA: Stanford University Press.

Wagner, R. K. (2003). Smart people doing dumb things: The case of managerial incompetence. In R. J. Sternberg (Ed.), *Why Smart People Can Be So Stupid* (pp. 42–63). New Haven, CT: Yale University Press.

Chapter 4

Sociability Dimension

> "If civilization is to survive, we must cultivate the science of human relationships—the ability of all peoples, of all kinds, to live together, in the same world at peace."
>
> — Letter from Franklin D. Roosevelt to
> Winston Churchill the day before Roosevelt died

Sociability is a person's fittedness to be in a society of others. Fittedness refers to a person's ability to be with others, and society refers to an established group or culture with set social norms of behavior.

A person who wants to be successful within a group often gives up individual or personal needs for the greater good of the group and its members. Therefore, the commission of a criminal act such as stealing or physical violence is not condoned because it is a social act that threatens the social cohesiveness of a group.

Some would say that common sense sees the connection between sociability and leadership. Leadership involves people interacting with others constantly—leaders attempt to get others to act, think, and feel in ways they may not ordinarily choose to.

When one examines the utilization of what is called a "360 degree" leadership assessment, a significant number of the survey items are social in nature. *360 degrees* is an attempt to evaluate a supervisor's, manager's, or leader's ability by surveying persons who work *under* them, *with* them, and *above* them, hence the term *360 degrees of evaluation.*

Some recent research on social power by Keltner, VanCleef, Chen, and Kraus (2008) investigates what the authors call "ultrasociality" as the key power within an organization. Ultrasociality is defined as the intense socializing nature of humans of the source of power that makes or breaks an

87

organization of people. They postulate that power is afforded to those individuals and strategic behaviors that relate to the advancing of a group as a whole. When those in power begin to negate the interests of the group they lead, their power loses force, conflict rises, and the organization starts to falter.

An example of ultrasociality is the concept of democracy as a form of governing. Democracy attempts to foster ultrasociality, because it allows for power checks and balances. It stresses the rule of law, freedom of speech, public assembly, civil and human rights, and advocacy for the masses through elected officials.

Some research that supports the power of ultrasociality was conducted by Rudolph Rummel, a political scientist who is cited in the book later. Rummel researched the relationship of 371 international wars that occurred between 1816 and 2005 in which at least 1,000 people were killed. He found that 205 of the wars were between nondemocratic nations and 166 were between democratic and nondemocratic nations. He found there were no wars between democratic nations.

Mr. Rummel concluded there were five reasons for the absence of war between democratic nations:

1. Well-established democracies do not make war on and rarely commit lesser violence against each other.

2. The more two nations are democratic the less likely war is, and there will be less violence between them.

3. The more democratic a nation is, the less severe its overall foreign violence is.

4. In general, the more democratic a nation is, the less likely it will have collective violence among its own people.

5. The more democratic a nation, the less "democide" (the murder of its own citizens) will be tolerated.

The above points explain the issue of why a democratic system of government would be less prone to war and violence.

Democracy as a concept is synonymous with "of the people, representative, popular, egalitarian, republican, self-governing, and autonomous," according to the *Oxford English Dictionary*.

In citing Rummel's research, democratic principles seem to stress ultrasociality because of historical influence on protecting human kind. Rummel's conclusion that democracies kill fewer of their own than nondemocracies and try to avoid conflict with others raises an interesting point about ultrasociality governing systems.

The authors of our Constitution were looking for a system of governing that protected individuals' rights, religious freedoms, and cultural freedoms. It appears that historically, democracies have done a better job of respecting human needs and rights. Respecting the needs and rights of others is a core principle of ultrasociality.

Leaders who are not social will have great difficulty managing an ultra-social organization. This inability to be social results in an inability to handle the social intensity, scrutiny, and complexity.

Below are some established facts regarding sociability:

Fact 1: Sociability requires talking to others.

Talking is the ability to use words in an appropriate way when relating to another. The following anonymous quote captures this principle:

> It's the little things we say that make or break the beauty of an average day. Hearts like doors will open with ease to very little keys. And don't forget that two of these are "Thank You" and "If You Please."

People basically talk their way through life to their betterment or detriment. Saying the right thing at the right time with great frequency increases one's chances for social success. For example, addressing someone you have just met with a casual phrase like "Hey girl" or "Hey boy" versus a formal one like "Excuse me, ma'am" or "Excuse me, sir" could produce significantly different reactions. "Hey boy/girl" would often be seen as demeaning by the person being spoken to, while "Excuse me sir/ma'am" would be seen as a respectful social approach.

Another example of potentially detrimental speech is the use of profanity (coarse or vulgar language), and it is seen by many as a reflection of the social and emotional status of a person. People who frequently use profanity are often perceived as less sophisticated and intelligent by those who rarely or do not use profanity.

Talking not only involves the appropriate use of words; it also involves verbal techniques. A verbal technique is the structuring of words to accomplish a certain goal. For example, asking questions is sometimes called an "interrogative," something used to gain information as knowledge from someone else. It is frequently used in everyday interaction. Asking someone "What time would you like to meet for dinner?" "How was your day?" or "Why did you leave so early?" are examples of interrogative verbal techniques.

Talking also reflects the nature of a relationship between two people. The terms *high* versus *low* form the nature of a relationship and refer to the formality of expected talk. Saying to someone, "Mr. Jones, we will be meeting at John's Steak House on 18 Baker Street at 7 p.m.," versus "Jonesy, I'll see you at the steak joint on Baker Street when you get there," indicates high versus low formality relationship.

Fact 2: Sociability requires not only the words that are expressed but the paralanguage used with the words.

Paralanguage refers to those aspects of talking that work with our words as they flow from our mouths. Paralanguage refers to voice tone, volume, or pitch. It also involves the number of words spoken per minute, the diversity of the words used in terms of syllables per word, the pauses between our words, and the cultural accent of our words.

For instance, tone of voice is viewed as a reflection of the emotional state of a person while they are speaking. The recognition of one's emotional state is important because it reflects the force or intention behind their words. Someone saying they are not angry in words but expressing anger in their tone is worth noting. Emotions that are intense can lead to actions that reflect that person's emotional state.

The absence of pauses between words and number of syllables (sounds) per word used is also worth noting. People who speak with few pauses between words and utilize diverse words are perceived as eloquent or well spoken. Eloquent individuals are seen as having power because their way of speaking reflects what is going on in the brain. This is why people who stutter have social difficulties—they are perceived as slow witted when in reality they are not.

Fact 3: The nonverbal aspects of relating are more important than the talking and paralanguage aspects.

Nonverbal refers to any human actions toward others that do not involve one's words or paralanguage, hence the term *nonverbal* (nonwords).

Nonverbal behavior involves *facial expression* (eyes, mouth, facial muscles); *body movement* (arms, hands, legs, feet, and posture); *body placement* (distance, proximity); *tactility* (touching); *chronemics* (timing); and *context* (environment and situational factors).

Most research reports that nonverbal actions account for between 60 to 70 percent of the variance in human interaction. In other words, you have a 60 to 70 percent chance of success or failure in social interactions based on your nonverbal competence.

Facial expression appears to be the most important of all the nonverbal factors. The theory is that prior to language sophistication, humans probably used facial expressions to communicate needs and thoughts. This is why the first action one engages in when sizing up a new person is to look at the individual's face.

For example, many cultures teach facial display rules to ensure proper etiquette. In these cultures one is to try and maintain a facial display that is positive or neutral. This is frequently exhibited in Asian and Native American cultures. On the other hand, there are many cultures that stress natural facial display rather than restrained display, as it conveys genuineness of emotion.

It appears the reason nonverbal communication is important is that it has several social functions in human interactions:

- It regulates human interactions because it provides people social cues (if they pay attention) when to start and stop talking—sometimes called turn taking. For example, when a person starts to slow down or pause while speaking, it indicates they are prepared for a response.

- It reflects information that is often not verbalized, such as how people are feeling or their attitude toward a topic of discussion. For instance, people may say they agree with a request made of them such as going out to dinner, yet their facial expression and voice tone indicate otherwise. This is important to notice because ignoring it can have negative social outcomes.

- It indicates social closeness or distance one has toward another. This can be critical when deciding when someone you are attracted to is or is not attracted to you.

- It determines the nature of a relationship as business or impersonal versus intimate or close.

- It can be used to convey or exert control or power over someone. Giving someone a raised eyebrow or intense eye contact reflects an attempt to exhibit social force.

Fact 4: Sociability requires focused attention to be successful.

Paying undivided attention to something is critical in understanding it and responding to it. You pay attention to something by focusing your senses. You focus your senses to become sensitive, which means to become aware. The more aware you are, the fewer mistakes you are prone to make. For example, the more you pay attention while driving your automobile (your actions and other drivers' actions), the less prone you are to becoming involved in an accident.

The above principle holds true in social interactions as well as relationships. The more aware you are of your own actions toward others and theirs toward you, the less prone you are to having a social accident.

Human beings have five sensory organs available to them—eyes, ears, nose, mouth, and skin. These organs produce the mechanisms that allow humans to see, hear, smell, taste, and touch. The extent to which and how these senses are used is dependent on one's culture.

The Western European view is primarily using one's eyes and ears to sense what is going on around them. Other cultures use their sense of smell as well as eyes and ears in social situations. Smell sense is important in cultures that do not stress deodorants since they believe a person's natural smell reflects who he or she is. Other cultures stress a lot of touching as a social behavior. Regardless of the senses used in a culture in social interactions, they are critical because they determine the degree of social awareness.

A modern phenomenon that has come about that threatens our sensory awareness is the proliferation of electronic forms of communication. Relating and relationships are increasingly being conducted via e-mail, text messaging, chat rooms, online dating, Facebook, and other electronic mechanisms.

The fallout from this is unknown, but this quote from Maggie Jackson's book *Distracted: The Erosion of Attention and the Coming Dark Age* (2008) indicates it may not be advantageous.

> A face to face, and soul, is harder to fathom and less predictable than a virtual encounter. By losing the will to face one another, we are meeting, which demands a mutual reading of body language, emotion turning away from the messy, unpredictable, and REAL in life. Virtual pink slips, condolences, courtship, custody visits, lovers' breakups—all relegated the *hard parts* of life to a thinner, indirect realm.

Fact 5: There is a phenomenon called *Social Channel Capacity* that determines the number of relationships we can handle.

Robin Dunbar, a British anthropologist, has done research on what he calls *Social Channel Capacity*. This concept refers to the ability one has in managing many relationships in their lives.

Dunbar states that human beings have the largest brains of any mammal based on their body size, followed by primates (apes, monkeys). Dunbar believes that brain size correlates with the group size within which one can live. For example, primate groups rarely reach a size of over 30 members. Humans, on the other hand, socialize in the largest groups of all primates because we have larger brains that allow us to handle the social complexity of larger groups.

When Dunbar studied 21 hunter-gatherer societies from the Walbiri in Australia to the Ammassalik in Greenland, the maximum size of any group was 148.4. This finding is supported elsewhere; for example, the Hutterites (a cultural/religious sect that has operated for hundreds of years) in North America have a strict policy that when a colony approaches 150, it splits in two—this suggests that when the number of people in a group becomes too large they split.

When groups reach sizes of above 150, Dunbar reports that they have to impose complex hierarchies, rules, laws, and other formal measures to command loyalty and minimize conflict. In smaller groups, order can be accomplished by developing personal loyalties and direct human-to-human contact. They do not need a complex legal system, policing system, etc., to control their members (Dunbar, 2010).

Fact 6: Sociability can be influenced by heredity.

There is significant research that all human abilities are influenced by one's heredity and biology. Athleticism, linguistics, mathematics, and musical and artistic abilities are influenced by genetics. Many children show early aptitude to be good at certain human abilities. One child is fascinated by numbers, another by words, another to body movement and related activities. This raises the debate of the power of nature (heredity and biology) over nurture (environmental exposure and learning).

Such research is usually done by what are called *twin studies.* Twin studies involve locating identical twins who have been raised apart from each other, and then analyzing their biological parents and nonsimilar environments. When these twins are discovered later in life, they are evaluated in terms of IQ scores, athleticism, social and emotional disposition, and other

94

criteria to determine their degree of similarity (concordance). The basis for this is that identical twins are monozygotic (one egg) and therefore genetically alike versus fraternal twins who are dizygotic (two eggs) and have different sets of genes.

A pair of identical twins share a remarkable physical similarity as well as other traits such as tone of voice and mannerisms. However, when one becomes well-acquainted with identical twins, differences will emerge.

These twin studies do conclude that heredity is an important aspect of people's personality traits and hence their social demeanor. Yet these identical twins also have some personality trait dissimilarities caused by the power of nurturing and environment. It appears that heredity can account for 30 to 50 percent of variability in various personality traits, but these traits are susceptible to change based on learning and one's environment (Segal, 2005).

Fact 7: Sociability is affected by a person's biological state.

In recent years, scientists have found a direct relationship between people's ability to socialize and their body chemistry. The human machine is run by chemistry and electricity. Everything the body does—from thinking to acting to feeling—is affected by chemical or electrical impulses. Malfunction in these chemical/electrical processes can create problems from a sociability standpoint.

One of the chemicals that is critical to human sociability is oxytocin. It is sometimes called the brain's "Golden Rule" switch for "friendly" behavior. Oxytocin is a catalyst for what could be described as pro-social behavior in humans and can be found in both men and women. Oxytocin is probably more prevalent in women because of the maternal/nurturing role required of women in the rearing of offspring; however, it is a critical sociability factor beyond maternity because it encourages friendly sociable behaviors in both males and females and increases paternalism in males.

Another chemical critical to sociability is vasopressin, which is necessary for socially aggressive behavior. Vasopressin can be a double-edged sword in that it promotes social aggression. Social aggression can be positive when it comes to parenting because it promotes a lack of fear of social encounters.

For example, setting limits on someone who is offending can require social aggressiveness on the part of the limit setter. Vasopressin can also trigger negative aggression from a social standpoint. If a person feels threatened by someone else, vasopressin can give the social will to be overly aggressive.

It is important to note that our understanding of sociability chemicals is still at an early stage scientifically. Yet knowing how certain chemicals affect sociability can help us in the future in treating social disorders such as shyness, introversion, sociopathy, and autism.

Fact 8: Sociability is strongly associated with physical health and mental health.

Membership in a large number of groups was once thought to be detrimental to one's health and well-being due to the many stressors that multiple relationships can cause. It appears the opposite is true. Just like diet and exercise are predictors of good health, sociability is also; several research studies demonstrate this.

A 2005 study by Professor Bernadette Boden-Albala at Columbia University found that socially isolated stroke victims were twice as likely to have another stroke within five years as those who had meaningful social relationships.

Researcher Karen Ertel's 2008 study, published in *American Journal of Public Health,* tracked 16,638 elderly Americans over a six-year period. The study found that there was significantly less memory loss in those elderly who were in socially active and healthy social networks.

A 2003 study at Carnegie Mellon University by Sheldon Cohen and his colleagues (published in *Psychosomatic Medicine)* found that people in diverse social networks were less susceptible to the common cold than people who are not as socially active. This is interesting because more diverse networks increase the number of germs a person can be exposed to.

A major factor in sociability and health is group identity or belonging to a group. A BBC prison study entitled "Rethinking Psychology of Tyranny" demonstrates this. In the study, male volunteers were assigned to one of two groups—"prisoners" or "guards"—in a simulated prison environment. After eight days into the experiment, the males assigned to the prisoner group developed a group identity against the guard group. The guard group did not develop a shared group identity against the prisoner group. The guard group began to experience social isolation from each other and obviously the prisoners.

The guard group eventually reported higher levels of emotional discomfort and added stress versus the prisoner group. For example, the cortisol levels in the guards were significantly higher (an indicator of increased stress) than in the prisoner group. The study concluded that social isolation can be detrimental to one's mental and physical well-being (Reicher & Haslam, 2006).

Fact 9: Social relationships can cause a social contagion that can be for better or worse. (It appears you should choose your friends carefully.)

It is well known that being around others can spread germs and therefore illness, hence the famous bubonic plague that devastated the populations of Europe. Can being around others spread not only physical diseases but conditions or habits such as obesity or smoking? Can being around others make us less prone to obesity and smoking? The answer appears to be yes on both counts.

Nicholas Christakis's and James Fowler's *Connected* (2009) presents findings on whether social networks have power and influence on certain aspects of our being. Some findings suggest that happiness is contagious and one's friends can make you fat or thin.

Christakis and Fowler have also found that our social networks underlie financial scams, eating disorders, substance abuse, suicide clusters, voter turnout, altruism, and even innovation. It appears we are unconsciously led by our friends and their friends to our benefit and detriment, and now there is science to support this.

Networks have been evaluated by electrical engineers studying power station connections, neuroscientists studying genetic networks, and physicists studying atom networks. They do this because networks are connections between phenomena that can affect other phenomena embedded in these networks.

The question is whether humans have a connectedness due to their need to socialize that supersedes their ability to be individuals and rise above the networks. The answer is most likely no. We are all highly susceptible to the influences of other networks.

In a study conducted by V. I. Clendenen, et al. (1994), the researchers found that people randomly assigned to be seated near strangers who eat a lot wind up doing the same, and the effect can be so subconscious that it has been called "mindless eating."

One way to measure obesity is body mass index (BMI). A normal BMI is considered to be 20 to 24. A BMI that is 25 to 29 is considered overweight, and a BMI that is 30 or above is obese. From 1990 to 2000, the percentage of obese people according to BMI increased from 21 percent to 33 percent. From 2000 to the present, the percentage of Americans who are obese (according to BMI) has reached 66 percent of the population. It appears this increase has direct connection to social contagion or connectedness.

Suicide can often occur in what appears to be a social contagion or connected phenomena. For example, in a small village in Manitoba, Canada, a suicide epidemic occurred—15 in 1995. The normal suicide rate for Manitoba is 14.5 cases per 100,000 people. In 1995, a suicide rate of 400 per 100,000 people occurred. Six people hung themselves in four months and another 19 attempted suicide (Wilkie, MacDonald, & Hildalh, 1998).

In 1994, concerns for media contagion and suicide led the Centers for Disease Control to suggest that the news media offer alternative ways of publicizing suicide occurrences. The CDC even went so far as to provide sample obituaries for journalists to control the potential of suicide contagion.

In Christakis's and Fowler's book, several hundred studies are reviewed supporting the power of social connectedness and its influence on our emotions, habits, physical health, and beliefs. It is probably important, therefore, to choose your friends wisely because their closeness to you may be more powerful than you may have previously considered both in terms of positive and negative effects.

Fact 10: Electronic communication is altering our social reality.

> "A face-to-face meeting, which demands a mutual reading of body language, emotion, and soul, is harder to fathom and less predictable than a virtual encounter. But by losing the will to face one another, we are turning away from the messy, unpredictable, and REAL in life. Virtual pink slips, condolences, courtship, custody visits, lovers' breakups—all relegated the hard parts of life to a thinner, indirect realm."
>
> — Jackson, 2008

Electronic social relationships are proliferating at such a rate that Nielsen Online reports that social networking is now the fourth most popular online activity. They report it is growing at three times the rate of overall Internet usage. This new wave of relating raises concerns about its benefits and risks and raises the question: *Does social networking lessen loneliness and boost self-esteem or does it have the opposite effect?*

John Cacioppo, co-author of *Loneliness: Human Nature and the Need for Social Connection* (2008), suggests that the use of social networking as a substitute for face-to-face interaction is futile and will ultimately be unfulfilling. A person who is "chatting" online can never really be sure who is on the other end of a virtual conversation and therefore gives a false sense of reality. Cacioppo and Patrick believe that social networking is an escape for those who cannot manage face-to-face relationships and will likely increase loneliness and other emotional and social problems.

Our need for interpersonal communication is basic to who we are as humans. According to Cacioppo, "We need face-to-face interaction because it is fundamental to what we are…. We need it to enrich our lives and the richness affects our brains."

A study conducted by Scott Caplan at the University of Delaware (as cited in DiSalvo, 2010) looked at people who prefer being online over face-to-face interaction and found that these individuals displayed socially anxious behavior and had greater obsessive compulsive tendencies such as playing video games, watching pornography, and gambling. Caplan added that he believes people drawn to online relationships will start using social networking as a form of addiction to regulate moods and their self-absorbed tendencies.

The research has also shown some positive effects of relating online, however. In a 2008 study of 477 Facebook® users, Cliff Lampe of Michigan State University found advantages of electronic relating, including increased social capital, i.e., having more relationships than one would normally have. Lampe states that being online helped those with low self-esteem because their ability increased their social capital, which increased their self-esteem (Lampe, Ellison, & Steinfield, 2008).

It could be the above result is due to the fact that socially anxious people could avoid visual, auditory, and nonverbal behaviors that face-to-face relating requires. In 2009, Patty Valkenburg of the University of Amsterdam, School of Communication (as cited in DiSalvo, 2010), found that membership in a social networking site helped adolescents. She concluded that the networking site built self-esteem by providing another method in friendship development.

It appears that this new means of sociability presents some interesting perspectives on the future of human relationships, both positive and negative. Much of the current research points to a more negative outcome due to the lack of real face-to-face relationships. This lack of real encounters may reinforce a greater tendency to avoid social realities that are necessary. They may also give people who have sociability difficulties a false sense of confidence. Conversely, social networking may be a place to test the social waters of relationships slowly so that those without social confidence can have relationships they may not otherwise have.

Developing and Applying Your Sociability

Attentive Ability

> "It is the province of knowledge to speak, and it is the privilege of wisdom to listen."
>
> – Oliver Wendell Holmes

Attentiveness is the first step in developing your sociability; it is the ability to utilize your eyes and ears constantly when interacting with others. It also involves using them consciously but not just constantly. Many of us are lazy when it comes to using these two senses. We take them for granted. The more you utilize your eyes and ears at a conscious level, the more "aware" you are. Awareness is a sign of intelligence.

Many of us have had the experience of driving an automobile. We do it without a lot of conscious effort because it is constant and a habit. Unfortunately when someone has had a close call while driving or is involved in an auto accident, he or she becomes more attentive (aware) so that it does not happen again.

Many of our social interactions have become habit, and we are not conscious of what's really going on. This is why many relationships we have fail because we become lazy in our day-to-day relationships. Unfortunately for many, this laziness causes a social accident. Some social accidents are irreparable, and we lose relationships that matter to us.

Attentiveness is also important because when people feel you are paying attention to them, they feel respected. This can create what is called "social reciprocity" between you and the person to whom you are paying attention. Social reciprocity is a fancy way of saying "you reap what you sow." People who are paid attention to tend to want to reciprocate by giving their attention to you.

The best way to be attentive is to utilize what are called good nonverbal skills. Nonverbal skills were discussed earlier in the book as a critical factor in sociability. Below are some nonverbal behaviors to consider when talking to someone:

1. Good eye contact when interacting

2. Appropriate facial display

3. Erect posturing

4. Appropriate hand and arm movement

5. Elimination of distractive mannerisms (such as hair twirling, tapping pens, typing on keyboard, looking at watch)

6. Appropriate distance between you and the person you are talking to

A person who has exemplified this dimension is Diane Sawyer.

Diane Sawyer—ABC News

Diane Sawyer's interviewing style draws people out because she is a good listener and highly attentive to those she's interviewing.

Sawyer's career as a broadcast journalist began after she served for several years as a Nixon administration press aide. Sawyer worked with Nixon as he repared his memoirs and also helped him prepare for his famous interview with David Frost. For some time, she was thought to be the source "Deep Throat" as the Watergate scandal unraveled (Diane Sawyer, n.d.).

Sawyer joined CBS in 1978, and from her first job as a State Department correspondent, Sawyer's career spring boarded from there at CBS. Eventually she left CBS in 1989 for ABC.

Her "sunny disposition" as an interviewer has always helped her secure better ratings, and she has earned a reputation for finding a balance between hard and soft news interviews (Lovdahl, n.d.).

Sawyer has interviewed world leaders, including an exclusive interview with President George W. Bush after the Hurricane Katrina debacle.

(continued)

She has proved capable of delivering on interviews with Boris Yeltsin, Iranian President Mahmoud Ahmadinejad, Fidel Castro, and the Clintons as well as interviews with Marla Maples, Michael Jackson, Madonna, and Britney Spears.

Sawyer once said, *"I think the one lesson I have learned is that there is no substitute for paying attention."*

Responsive Ability

"Only a life lived for others is a life worth living."

– Albert Einstein

Responsiveness is the ability to mirror or mimic back to someone using your nonverbal and verbal communication as a display of social synchrony.

Social synchrony is similar to attentiveness in the sense that when you are being attentive to the person talking to you, he or she may perceive you are in sync with what he or she is saying. Responsiveness, on the other hand, requires that you consciously try to show *in your actions and words* that you are in sync with the other person.

Human interaction is like dancing with someone. When two people are dancing together step-by-step, without hesitation, a social chemistry or bonding begins to occur. If the dancing partners are out of step with each other though, there is a discomfort, hesitation, and possibly a cessation of the dance.

When two people are walking down the street together while conversing, they usually try to maintain the same pace of movement with each other. If one person walks ahead of the other, the interaction can become strained.

Nonverbal responsiveness is frequently displayed by utilization of synchronized facial expressions. If someone you are speaking with is happy and it is conveyed on his or her face, then you should display happiness in your face. Conversely, if someone is unhappy, you might want to convey a face of sadness or concern that reflects the other person's state of mind. The mutual display of synchronized facial expression can be socially powerful.

Of course there are many other ways to show nonverbal synchrony. Some are listed below:

- Someone waves to you and you reciprocate by waving back.

- Someone puts his or her hand out to shake yours, and you reciprocate by extending your hand.

- Someone is struggling while carrying something heavy such as furniture, and you attempt to help him or her by grabbing one side of the furniture.

Responsiveness can also be displayed verbally. One of the most common ways to respond verbally is to repeat what someone has said to you for clarification that you heard him or her correctly. This does several things. First, it lets the other person know you heard him or her. Second, it keeps the conversation on track because it allows the person who is speaking to stay on track with you. Third, it allows you as the listener to retain what you heard because you are repeating back to the speaker.

Sometimes people comment that this repeating back can be distracting to the speaker. To avoid this, do not repeat what the person has said word-for-word, but summarize or paraphrase your reflective response. Second, do not repeat everything someone says to you because that is distracting. A good place to use a reflective verbal response is if someone has been speaking to you for a long period of time (2 to 3 minutes/about 400 words).

Responsiveness can also be conveyed by asking relevant questions, which are those that connect content or subject matter being discussed by the other while one is listening. For example, if someone is discussing a problem he or she is having at work regarding a promotion or pay raise, an irrelevant question would be one that completely changes the subject such as "How long have you owned that car you're driving?"

Many of our day-to-day conversations are not synchronized but constantly go off on tangential subjects and content that are not connected to each other. It is not that changing the subject of a conversation is wrong;

there are many instances where it would be appropriate due to time constraints or interruptions that force the change.

A person who has exemplified this dimension is Sidney Poitier.

Sidney Poitier—Actor

Sidney Poitier's verbal and nonverbal presence as an actor on and off screen has been the key to his success—you are drawn to his presence.

Poitier's rise to fame as an actor came about during turbulent times in America. He came to New York City when he was 15 (he was born in Miami but was raised in the Bahamas) and looked to acting as a way to earn a living.

Poitier had trouble at first finding roles because he could not read very well and had a Bahamian accent. He also had difficulty finding roles that did not play to stereotypes. Eventually he landed roles that made him a leading man; he never played a subordinate. His success drew great praise from the African-American community, while some whites were uncomfortable with his status.

One of his most controversial roles was the lead in "Guess Who's Coming to Dinner," where Poitier played a black doctor whose fiancé is white. Eventually Poitier changed the image of African-American actors—he proved he could be a serious dramatic actor and romantic lead, and in the process personified African Americans' struggle for equality. Poitier said of his performances, *"I was saying to an audience, this is who I am; look at me."* ("Sidney Poitier Biography—Academy of Achievement," (2009).

Reflectiveness Ability

> "Compassion will cure more sins than condemnation."
>
> – Henry Ward Beecher

To reflect socially means to think about, consider, or give thought to what is going on inside a person with whom you are talking. Much of our behavior, especially when we were younger, is primarily selfish. We are not likely to reflect on another person's needs, wants, feelings, ways of thinking, or values. It is primarily about ourselves. This is probably driven by our innate self-preservation instincts to survive.

Initially, if we have loving parents, they will ensure our survival and make sure our needs to survive are met. As we get older, usually during adolescence, we will seek our independence and strive not to be dependent on our parents. Adolescence is probably the most selfish stage of human development.

Some of us grow out of this earlier than others and realize we need others. This stage could be called interdependence during our development. Most societies try to stress this by calling it teamwork. People need people and must work in teams as a means of survival. Some evolutionary psychologists believe that this sense of teamwork enables human kind to eventually control its survival over other species.

The fourth stage could possibly be called "dependent" upon. This usually occurs when humans become parents and they have helpless offspring needing them for their survival. Being successful as parents necessitates what could be called "selflessness." Selflessness is prioritizing others over yourself. Meeting the needs of others becomes critical. This stage requires "reflective" abilities.

Reflectiveness requires "empathy" for others. A mentor of mine stated that empathy was the core condition for a society's survival. Without empathy, he believed societies eventually would destroy themselves.

Empathy is the capacity to place yourself in another person's frame of reference. When you are empathizing with another, you are asking yourself, "how would I feel, think, or act if this were happening to me?"

Empathy should not be confused with sympathy. Of course to have sympathy or compassion for another requires empathy. Yet one can empathize with someone without sympathizing. For example, if a teenager were to receive a bad grade on an exam because he or she chose to go out with friends the night before the exam, the teenager could be shown empathy but not sympathy.

You could say to that teenager, "I know when you are in high school being with your friends is more important to you than school (empathy) yet you flunked the exam and now you have to work twice as hard to get your average up" (no sympathy). You would be saying to the teenager, "I can understand why you did what you did, but now you have to pay for it."

Sympathy refers to sharing the thoughts, feelings, and resulting actions of those thoughts and feelings. Empathy is when you can understand and respect the thoughts and feelings behind their actions, but you cannot ally yourself with the actions those thoughts and feelings produce. With empathy you can still be held accountable.

Empathy is a powerful ability when applied to sociability, because when you give empathy you tend to get it in return. It is human to err or make mistakes. The problem is people who are not shown empathy tend to deny their mistakes or flaws and blame others or circumstances for those mistakes. Consequently, they often tell themselves that when things go well, they themselves are responsible, but when things go wrong, it is someone else's responsibility.

A person who has exemplified this dimension is Charles Gibson.

Charles Gibson—former news anchor for ABC News

Charles Gibson's demeanor both on his news broadcasts and his interviews reflected a "genuine" ability to empathize with people, which was critical to his audience appeal.

Charles ("Charlie") Gibson worked for ABC news from 1975 in numerous capacities until his retirement in 2009. He worked his way up from general assignment reporter to "Good Morning America" anchor to "World News Tonight" anchor.

Gibson's style both on news broadcasts and during interviews has been called genuine. He was praised by *The New York Times* for his reporting on the Virginia Tech shootings, where he showed empathy while moving the story forward. *The New York Times* op-ed further said that Gibson was (at that time) becoming "the nation's news anchor," mainly because he refrained from inserting too much emotion but was simultaneously kind and straightforward (Stanley, 2007).

At the conclusion of a broadcast where the 32 Virginia Tech shooting victims were shown in photographs, Gibson said, *"Those are the faces to remember."*

Prosocial Ability

> "No-one becomes rich without enriching others."
>
> – Andrew Carnegie

Social interaction can probably be divided into four broad categories: *prosocial*, *social*, *asocial*, and *antisocial*. Prosocial behavior refers to human interactions that are promoted or initiated with the goal of helping another. These behaviors involve a genuine concern for the feelings, thoughts, and needs that people in our lives are experiencing. Examples of prosocial behavior would be volunteering your time, taking part in charitable causes, or just assisting others without any monetary reward for doing so. Terms such as *altruism* or *selflessness* are often associated with prosocial thinking and actions.

Social behavior refers to human relationships or interactions that are comfortable and businesslike. These behaviors involve minimal emotional investment in your daily interactions. People in customer service roles are required to exhibit to others social behaviors that are friendly, nonargumentative, and courteous. On a daily basis, being polite or courteous to strangers would also be an example of social behavior.

Asocial behavior refers to noninteractive behavior. People who exhibit asocial behavior avoid interactions with others because they cause a high degree of discomfort or anxiety. Sometimes *hermit, recluse,* or *solitary* are terms associated with asocial behavior. People who are shy or introverted will exhibit asocial behaviors. The asocial person, unlike the antisocial person described next, does not dislike people but would rather avoid interaction altogether.

The antisocial category refers to persons who exhibit behaviors toward others that are harmful. Fighting, arguing, or deviousness toward others are characteristic of antisocial behaviors. Criminality would be considered the ultimate type of antisocial behavior because it has no regard for the feelings, thoughts, or needs of others. Harming others is the result.

When considering the above four categories of social behavior, it is important to note that many of us have and will exhibit all four of these types of social behavior in our lives. We will exhibit these behaviors because they are influenced by a variety of factors such as environmental circumstances, social rules, ethnic and cultural norms, and relationship history. For example, the social role and environmental circumstances of police officer or soldier place the individual in situations where harming another is probably inevitable. On the other hand, the social role of a doctor or minister places the individual in situations that do not promote harming others. Another example is someone who has a poor relationship history with you. He or she might have abused the relationship by not being trustworthy.

A major controversy in warfare is the treatment of prisoners who may have information that could help their captors prevent harm or death to others. Some would argue that antisocial approaches—threatening them and depriving them of certain needs—are justified in securing critical information. On the other hand, others would argue that utilizing prosocial approaches such as being kind and fair and meeting their needs would be more appropriate in securing critical information.

Prosocial leadership would advocate that all of the social skills discussed in this chapter—attentiveness, responsiveness, and reflectiveness—should be applied when interacting with others, no matter what the environmental circumstances, social roles, ethnic and cultural norms, and relationship history might be.

Prosocial leadership does advocate holding people accountable when they are wrong, defending oneself if threatened, and protecting the rights of others from antisocial actions. It means that prosocial actions should be practiced as much as the social circumstances allow and returned to when proven direct harm to self and others is not imminent.

A person who has exemplified this dimension is Franklin Delano Roosevelt.

Franklin Delano Roosevelt—former United States President

In photographs and interviews, Franklin Delano Roosevelt (FDR) displayed a prosocial demeanor. His son and grandson described him as being that way no matter the circumstances.

It was likely FDR's "first-rate temperament" (so labeled by Supreme Court Justice Oliver Wendell Holmes) and optimism, as well as his emotional maturity, which was testimony of his compassion for others, that allowed him to pursue his New Deal agenda and seek assistance for plain folks, the "forgotten man," and that "third of the nation, ill-housed, ill-clad, and ill-nourished" that suffered so greatly during the Great Depression.

(continued)

Rather than letting extreme external circumstances like polio affect what was, by all accounts, an incredibly optimistic nature from boyhood onward, FDR endeavored to be the public servant he had always wanted to be.

FDR used his fire-side chats to communicate his hopes for the nation in a calm, yet strong manner. *"The test of our progress is not whether we add more to the abundance of those who have much; it is whether we provide enough for those who have too little,"* Roosevelt said.

Sociability Test

Let's measure your sociability potential.

Below are some actions that measure your sociability skills. Rate the statements honestly. Use the following scale and place a check (✓) in the box to rate yourself for each statement.

1 = Rarely   2 = Sometimes   3 = Usually   4 = Often   5 = A Lot

You may want to ask some people who know you well to rate you, using the same scale. See how closely your score and their scores match. Don't be surprised if there is a big difference.

	1	2	3	4	5
1. I pay close attention to the person's facial expressions while talking with them.	❏	❏	❏	❏	❏
2. I listen to the person I'm talking to without interrupting them no matter how long it takes them to say what they have to say.	❏	❏	❏	❏	❏
3. I shut off my cell phone or computer when someone approaches me to talk about something that needs my undivided attention.	❏	❏	❏	❏	❏

	1	2	3	4	5
4. I try to maintain appropriate eye contact when talking to someone one on one when I sense they need my attention.	❏	❏	❏	❏	❏
5. I am conscious of what my body movements (hands, arms, legs, etc.) are doing while talking with someone.	❏	❏	❏	❏	❏
6. When someone has made a mistake in front of me and they seem ashamed or embarrassed, I tend to look in another direction and act like nothing has happened.	❏	❏	❏	❏	❏
7. I think it is important to consider the feelings of others as well as their thoughts.	❏	❏	❏	❏	❏
8. I will keep my emotions in check when someone is angry with me.	❏	❏	❏	❏	❏
9. I am the first to apologize to someone whom I have hurt.	❏	❏	❏	❏	❏
10. When something goes wrong between myself and another, I quickly consider what I might have done to contribute to it.	❏	❏	❏	❏	❏

Scoring:

Add your total score and multiply the total by 2. This number is your ability potential in this dimension. For example: 30 × 2 = 60% ability in this range.

A score above 80% is a good score.

A score above 90% is an excellent score.

Note: A more accurate assessment of your ability in this dimension, which consists of 40 statements/questions versus the 10 shown in this book, can be found at www.sotelligence.com.

References

Boden-Albala, B., et. al. (2005). Social isolation and outcomes post stroke. *Neurology, 64*(11), 1888–1892.

Cacioppo, J. T., & Patrick, W. (2008). *Loneliness: Human nature and the need for social connection.* New York: W. W. Norton & Company.

Christakis, N. A., & Fowler, J. H. (2009). *Connected: The surprising power of our social networks and how they shape our lives.* New York: Little, Brown and Company.

Clendenen, V. I., Herman, C. P., & Polivy, J. (1994). Social facilitation of eating among friends and strangers. *Appetite, 23*(1), 1–13.

Cohen, S. (2003). Emotional style and susceptibility to the common cold. *Psychosomatic Medicine, 65*(4), 652–657. doi: 10.1097/ 01.PSY.0000077508.57784.DA

Diane Sawyer. (n.d.). *Wikipedia, the free encyclopedia.* Retrieved December 16, 2010, from http://en.wikipedia.org/wiki/Diane_Sawyer

DiSalvo, D. (2010). Are social networks messing with your head? *Scientific American Mind, 20*(7), 48–55.

Dunbar, R. I. (2010). *How many friends does one person need? Dunbar's number and other evolutionary quirks* (pp. 21–34). Cambridge, MA: Harvard University Press.

Ertel, K. A., Glymour, M. M., & Berkman, L. F. (2008). Effects of social integration on preserving memory function in a nationally representative U.S. elderly population. *American Journal of Public Health, 98*(7), 1215–1220. doi: 10.2105/AJPH.2007.113654

Jackson, M. (2008). *Distracted: The erosion of attention and the coming Dark Age.* Amherst, NY: Prometheus Books.

Keltner, D., VanCleef, G. A., Chen, S., & Kraus, M. W. (2008). Reciprocal influence model of social power. Emerging principles and lines of inquiry. *Advances in Experimental Social Psychology, 40,* 151–192.

Lampe, C., Ellison, N., and Steinfield, C. (2008). Changes in participation and perception of Facebook. ACM Conference on Computer Supported Cooperative Work. November 8–12. San Diego, CA.

Lovdahl, L. T. (n.d.). Sawyer, Diane. *The Museum of Broadcast Communications.* Retrieved December 16, 2010, from http://www.museum.tv/eotvsection.php?entrycode=sawyerdiane

Reicher, S., & Haslam, S. A. (2006). Rethinking the psychology of tyranny: The BBC prison study. *British Journal of Social Psychology*, *45*(1), 1–40. doi: 10.1348/014466605X48998

Segal, N. L. (2005). *Indivisible by two: Lives of extraordinary twins.* Cambridge, MA: Harvard University Press.

Sidney Poitier Biography—Academy of Achievement. (2009, July 31). *Academy of Achievement Main Menu.* Retrieved December 16, 2010, from http://www.achievement.org/autodoc/page/poi0bio-1

Stanley, A. (2007, April 19). Amid chaos, one notably restrained voice. *The New York Times.*

Wilkie, C., MacDonald, S., & Hildalh, K. (1998). Community case study: Suicide cluster in a small Manitoba community. *Canadian Journal of Psychiatry*, *43*(8), 823–828.

Chapter 5

Emotionality Dimension

> "Our emotions must be in the right amount, proportional to the event that called them forth; they must be expressed at the right time, in a way that is appropriate to the emotional trigger and circumstances in which it occurred; and they must be expressed in the right way, in a way that does no harm."
>
> — Artistotle, "The Temperate Person"

Emotionality, from a leadership perspective, is the ability to understand and utilize one's own emotions and the emotions of others in a constructive way. Emotions are powerful, because they "e" (to) motion (move) us to act or not act. Emotions are the foundations for our motivations. They are the fuel for our action, and without them we would appear lifeless.

Science has struggled with how to define and measure emotions. They are not something you can see directly with a microscope, X-ray, or MRI. They can be very fleeting. Some scientists believe that a single emotion can occur as rapidly as a quarter of a second in our bodies (Ekman, 2003).

The study of emotions as a scientific phenomenon is in its infant stages, maybe just 30 years old. Daniel Goleman's book *Emotional Intelligence,* published in 1995, was probably the first book to bring the study of emotions to the public's attention. It was a best-seller.

Since Goleman's book, there have been a series of books written on emotions. Many of them focus on specific types of emotions such as *Authentic Happiness* by Martin Seligman; *Loneliness: Human Nature and the Need for Social Connection* by John Cacioppo and William Patrick; and *The Emotional Brain* by Joseph LeDoux.

115

Paul Ekman's book *Emotions Revealed* examines the emotions of fear, anger, sadness, disgust, and happiness from a cross-cultural perspective. Ekman seeks to find out whether there are universal rules for how emotions are experienced and revealed cross-culturally, and his cumulative research has revealed that emotions are universally experienced and expressed despite one's culture.

John Gottman's research on *The Mathematics of Marriage* is probably one of the first attempts to quantify emotional expressions between couples. Gottman, who has a degree in mathematics from MIT and went on to earn a Ph.D. in Psychology, developed a system called **SPAFF** (Specific Affect Coding System), which codes verbal and nonverbal information to identify emotions. Using this data, Gottman has been able to predict divorce with 90 percent accuracy within 15 years. If Gottman's research is correct, it appears emotional cues are critical at predicting relationship success or failure, at least within couples (Gottman, 2005).

Based on the above books and a review of the scientific literature, the following are some established facts about emotions.

Fact 1: Emotions can affect our thinking and actions in a negative way.

Emotions can affect our ability to think logically because they bias the way we think. Drew Westen's research in what he calls "confirmation bias" has found that people will discard facts that do not support their feelings and pursue facts that do (Westen, 2007). In other words, if we have taken a position or stand on a political issue, the only facts we will contemplate are the facts that support our feelings for that issue. It can be said that our feelings will most likely cause us to never take on opposing views on what we already believe.

Emotions from the past can also hijack our actions in present situations. If we have had a bad experience such as a divorce, combat experience, or a life threatening event that has intense negative emotions attached to it, we will often experience those intense negative emotions in the present. This is sometimes referred to as post traumatic stress reaction. A post (prior) traumatic (wound) stress (intense negative emotion) will reappear (reaction) in the present if the present event has several cues that the prior event had. For example, if a person who has previously experienced a very bitter divorce where infidelity was the root cause experiences similar circumstances in a new relationship, that person will experience those intense negative feelings so rapidly, that he or she will act on those feelings and accuse his or her current partner of infidelity. These infidelity perceptions may have no basis in fact in the current relationship, but the perception is caused by prior hurtful emotions.

Fact 2: We can communicate to others emotions that we had no intention of doing so.

I mentioned John Gottman's research in *The Mathematics of Marriage* above. Gottman measured one emotion per second that the couples were sending to each other at an unconscious level. Despite their lack of conscious awareness, each couple was sensing/receiving negative emotions that were gradually destroying their relationships. A lot of what affects us is below our conscious ability to sense (see, hear, taste, smell, touch). We cannot literally see viruses or bacteria that invade our bodies and make us ill, for example.

This phenomenon can occur for a couple of reasons. The first reason is our inability to see ourselves as others see us. In David Dunning's book *Self-Insights,* he reports that people's sense of their social skills is around 8.5 percent accurate and around 91.5 percent inaccurate (Dunning, 2005). In other words, there is slightly more than a 90 percent chance we do not see ourselves accurately in terms of our social ability.

Another reason we are not consciously aware is that most of us have not trained our eyes and ears to intently focus on what's going on in a human interaction. Most of us are on a type of automatic pilot in our day-to-day interactions with our established relationships. Our social interactions take on patterns of habits when we have been with someone over a period of time. Some of the social interaction habits can become destructive at an unconscious level, and they gradually erode the relationship.

Fact 3: Many of our emotional reactions are preprogrammed due to our instincts and ancestry.

Many human emotions such as anger, fear, jealousy, and disgust are prewired or instinctual. For example, most young children will experience frustration/ anger when they are forced to control their basic instincts such as eating or going to the bathroom. Teaching a child to delay their need for immediate gratification requires rewiring (parenting) their emotional responses. This is called "delayed gratification" or "impulse control."

This pattern of emotional control over our instinctual drives continues throughout our lifetime. Jealousy, for example, is a normal emotion for most of us if we see someone we love showing interest in another and that other person is a potential rival for our affection.

The development over time of our emotional reactions due to natural instincts is called emotional maturation. Spoiling children by providing the ability to get their needs met without much resistance can interfere with the emotional maturity process.

Another step in this emotional maturity process is when one achieves power; this power can potentially cause regression back to emotional immaturity. Power can often cause those that have it a false sense of having no emotional accountability. The more power one attains, the more he or she gets their way. This new power can begin to spoil the individual emotionally. A well-known study found that many people who achieved significant power begin to use drugs, indulge themselves in food and drink, and become more sexually aggressive. Some would call this a regression back to primal instincts (Neumarkt, 2005).

Fact 4: Facial expression is considered by science to be one of the best indicators of a person's emotional state.

In Paul Ekman's book *Unmasking the Face,* he states the human face is capable of 7,000 or more distinct expressions that have different meanings. For example, Ekman reports the human face has 19 different types of smiles, but only one is the genuine smile or truly happy smile. The other smiles are not necessarily fake but not as heart felt. He calls the genuine smile the

Duchenne smile, after a neurologist in the late 1800s who coined the term (Ekman & Friesen, 2003).

Silvan Tomkins, a scientist who influenced Paul Ekman's research on the face, claimed that facial expressions were innate and universal to our species no matter what culture we came from. In other words, facial expressions and the emotions they reflected were the same cross-culturally (Tomkins, Demos, & Smith, 1995).

A factor that influences facial expression and emotionality is a phenomenon coined by Ekman called *facial display rules.* Some cultures teach their children to control their facial displays because they reveal emotions so easily. By controlling facial displays, we show social etiquette and manners as well as regulating the power of emotions—especially destructive ones. These facial display rules are common in Asian culture and Native American cultures. It appears these cultures respected the social power of emotions reflected in the face (Ekman & Friesen, 2003).

In Albert Mehrabian's research on nonverbal communication, he reported that facial expression accounted for 55 percent of the variance in human communication versus 38 percent for voice tone and the remaining 7 percent being the words themselves. Based on his research, Mehrabian believed that facial displays mattered most in determining the outcome of social encounters with people (Mehrabian, 1971). This is probably why certain cultures stress facial display rules as a form of etiquette.

Another reason to consider the power of facial display and emotion is a phenomenon called *emotional contagion.* We all can feel the emotions that others feel, especially if we have a close relationship to them. If we do not care about them or do not identify with them, it may not occur at all or not at the same intensity. On the other hand, if a stranger were to display anger toward us through his face, it could trigger a similar intense emotion of anger in ours (Cacioppo & Patrick, 2008). This is probably why road rage experts state that if you have offended another driver while driving, do not look at the other driver if he or she pulls up beside you. It could intensify the other driver's anger and aggression toward you, especially if you give an angry look back.

Fact 5: The human voice is another very reliable indicator of a person's emotional state.

The scientist Silvan Tomkins mentioned above believed that the impulse to make a sound whenever an emotion is aroused is innate. He believed it was hard to keep signs of what is felt out of the voice, and each sound is different for each emotion. Many mothers with small infants say that every infant's cry is different in terms of its needs. One cry means it is hungry, another means it is hurting, and another means it is tired and so forth (Tomkins, Demos, & Smith, 1995). The infant does not have language skills, but its voice tone is its words. A DVD set entitled *Dunstan's Baby Language* describes this (Dunstan Baby, director, 2006).

The voice rarely gives false emotional messages whereas the face can, according to Tomkins and other researchers. This is because the voice is not regulated by muscles as the face is. The human face has 47 muscles, and these muscles can be trained to regulate expression. This is possibly why the voice is seen as more reliable.

The voice also captures our attention more than the face when sending emotions. A good example is listening to music. It is the voice of the singer that captures us emotionally more than the face. Of course the facial display has to match the voice of the singer in terms of emotion for us to listen if the performance is live. When we listen to music on the radio or from a CD, etc., we have no ability to see the face. It is the voice that captures our feelings.

Fact 6: Emotions are universally felt and expressed in all cultures.

It was initially believed that our emotional responses and gestures were socially learned and culturally influenced. Silvan Tomkins wrote two books on emotion and facial expression, and he proposed they were innate and universal regardless of culture.

Subsequent research by Paul Ekman and others confirms a universal language of emotional expression. The research studies in Ekman's *Emotions Revealed* found that expression of emotion was consistent across cultures.

As mentioned in Fact 4 above, Ekman also pointed out that some cultures may attempt to control emotional expression through what he called *display rules.* These display rules are socially learned as a form of social etiquette. Within many of these cultures that stress display rules, Ekman found that the social setting influenced the degree to which emotional expression was used. For example, Ekman found that Japanese subjects, normally known for strict facial display rules, displayed more natural emotional expression if they were not in a public setting (Ekman & Friesen, 2003).

Perhaps cultures that stress display rules for emotional expression realize the emotional contagion effect. Our human tendency to feel what other people feel can have negative consequences as well as positive. For example, if one person conveys an expression of anger on his or her face toward another, that other person can become angry in return. In another situation, if someone expresses fear in a crisis, those around him or her may become fearful, and a mass panic can take place.

Fact 7: There appears to be five basic emotions that are universal to all human beings.

There is good scientific evidence that there are five emotions that all humans experience regardless of culture. They are sadness, fear, anger, disgust, and happiness. The other emotions that we experience as humans are probably blends of the above due to social learning and societal development (Ekman, 2003).

Examples of such blends are the emotions *shame* and *guilt,* which are related to disgust. Disgust is an emotion that causes us to have an aversion to or repugnance for something that may not be good for our well-being. The emotions of shame and guilt are probably moderate forms of disgust because they help us develop aversions to things that are not good for us. Being disgusted with yourself for doing something that harmed you or another may prevent a similar experience in the future.

Fact 8: The basic emotions are needed for our survival despite the problems they cause.

The basic emotions of sadness, fear, anger, disgust, and happiness all have a relationship to our survival as well as our eventual demise.

Fear is needed to protect us from harming ourselves. Fearing the consequences of driving too fast, driving while under the influence, or doing something criminal, for example, can prevent us from taking part in such activities. Of course we can also become fearful of things we should not, and these are called irrational fears.

Anger is needed to protect us because it can motivate us to fight for self-preservation. Anger can also motivate us to find the strength to not give up under difficult circumstances. If we become angry at ourselves because we have become overweight due to a lack of exercise or poor eating, that anger may drive us to exercise and eat properly. Of course anger has significant potential dangers because it can motivate us to do things to harm others, which, in turn, may harm ourselves as well.

Sadness can be a positive emotion because it can force us to stop and think if we lose something of value. If I am sad because I lost a relationship with someone I cared about, it may prevent me in the future from doing things that contributed to losing another relationship. If a partner in a past relationship continually told me that I never listen or give him or her attention, I may be likely not to do those things in a future relationship. Of course chronic sadness can lead to depression, which is not beneficial.

Happiness is obviously important because it is a positive emotion to begin with. Happiness is an emotion that motivates us to do positive things. It is an emotion that gives us a passion for living. Happy people tend to be more optimistic, generous, and kind to others. Many people see finding happiness as life's purpose. The United States Constitution states that every human being has the right to pursue life, liberty, and happiness.

Disgust, as mentioned above, can be self-preserving, because it can teach us to avoid harmful things or actions. If I develop a disgust for the dangers of smoking or the abuse of alcohol, it could obviously be life-preserving. If I find it disgusting to neglect children, it may cause me to ensure that I will not allow children, particularly my own, to be abused. In this way, disgust motivates me to avoid harm being done to others as well as myself.

Fact 9: Emotional maturity and having a conscience are interconnected.

The concept of developing a conscience in humans is critical to long-term human survival. In a complex society, conscience is an ability to know right from wrong. Our conscience is heavily influenced by what might be called moral emotions. Guilt is a moral emotion in having a conscience, because it can prevent us from doing harm to others. Compassion is a moral emotion that is conscious driven because it is concerned with the needs of another versus oneself. Empathy is an emotion of conscience because it takes into account another person's emotions before one acts.

Guilt, compassion, and empathy can also be described as mature emotions because they may not be intuitive and must be nurtured and developed in children. Children are innately inclined to be angry, sad, fearful, disgusted, and happy because these emotions are basic to their survival. Moral emotions are not basic; they are developed in children through parenting and education.

Some children may be more *or* less capable of learning moral emotions because they have a genetic predisposition to do so. Genetics has a heavy influence in every aspect of our being. That is well documented. This is probably why some individuals simply cannot learn moral emotions despite every attempt by society to teach them. Such people are often labeled as sociopaths or psychopaths. They appear incapable of concern for others, and they are responsible for a significant amount of the crime in our society.

Moral emotion development can also be heavily influenced by environmental factors as well as genetics. Broken homes, drug abuse, poverty, and other environmental factors can also contribute to a lack of conscience or moral emotion development (Shermer, 2005).

Fact 10: Emotions often begin so quickly that we are not aware of their influence on our thinking and actions.

Emotions can come on as quickly as one quarter of a second. This quickness can be positive if we are threatened by something and that quick reaction protects us. This is probably why nature enabled us to experience emotions so quickly.

The flipside of this is that we may experience an emotion quickly that is irrational. In other words, there is no threat to our well-being, but we react as if there is. This is common in what is called post traumatic stress disorder (PTSD).

PTSD occurs frequently in soldiers who have experienced a need to be hyper-vigilant or aware in combat situations. This hyper-vigilance is really emotional sensitivity that is programmed into a soldier for his/her survival. In combat situations, reaction time is everything. A noise or visual cue in the environment is an emotional trigger to react quickly.

Unfortunately, our quick emotional reactions do not allow for mental processing (rational thinking). Often our reactions are unnecessary because there is no real threat to our existence once we have time to think. This is often called an irrational response because if we could have been rational we would not have reacted the way we did. Many individuals have said, "If I could have had time to think, I would have never said or did what I did." This is the danger of our innate ability to experience emotion so quickly.

We do not have to have been in combat and develop PTSD to be emotionally over-reactive. That is an extreme form. We all have experienced milder forms of our emotions being a trigger to doing something irrational. It happens every day to all of us; it is what makes us human.

Developing and Applying Your Emotionality

Identification Ability

> "It takes courage to know when one ought to be afraid."
>
> – James A. Michener

Identification is the ability to recognize emotional states in oneself and others quickly. It was stated above that our and others' emotions can occur as quickly as a half second. This quickness often causes us to act and think in irrational ways because our brain cannot analyze a situation as quickly.

A way to counter this is to develop an ability to quickly identify emotions within ourselves and others. This can be done by first developing what could be called an emotional vocabulary. An emotional vocabulary consists of words that describe emotions one is experiencing rapidly.

For example, how many words can you write down that describe various states of anger in 60 seconds? If you were able to write down between six and eight, that is very good. For example, here is my 60-second sample list: *furious, rage, aggravated, irritated, miffed, annoyed, bothered, ticked.* Now write yours without using any of mine. My guess is that it was not easy. That is because most of us are not emotionally "eloquent"; that is, we are not emotionally well-spoken.

In your emotional identification test, you will be asked to rate yourself on emotional identification in other ways besides vocabulary development. The key to emotional identification is to develop what scientists call *rapid cognition.* This is an ability to become quickly (rapid) aware (cognition). In professional baseball, for example, a hitter who is trying to hit a 95-mile-per-hour fast ball from 60 feet has less than a quarter of a second to react (swing/don't swing). A hitter learns to develop this ability by constant practice and repetition.

A person who has exemplified this dimension is Norman Schwarzkopf.

Norman Schwarzkopf—Commander, Operation Desert Storm

Gen. Norman Schwarzkopf had a long military career and won many accolades. His greatest achievement, perhaps, was his successful command of Operation Desert Shield and the subsequent Operation Desert Storm.

For all his successes as a leader given his abilities, Schwarzkopf never undervalued losing men and women in battle. Schwarzkopf said, *"To be a good leader you have to lead passionately. And I'm a passionate person. I feel very, very strongly about things. I'm an emotional person. The tragedy*

(continued)

of losing young men and women's lives is tough enough to swallow. To find out that it was preventable, is even tougher." ("Norman Schwarzkopf Interview—Academy of Achievement," 2007).

When Barbara Walters interviewed Schwarzkopf after Desert Storm, he teared up during the interview discussing this very matter of losing soldiers. For Schwarzkopf, showing emotion, whether sadness or fear, is not a sign of weakness. In another interview, Schwarzkopf said that being fearful makes you focused and then lets you see things in sharper focus.

Expression Ability

> "Always be a little kinder than necessary."
>
> – Sir James M. Barret

The expression of emotions is the ability to convey to others how you feel in a constructive manner. This does not mean that every emotion you experience has to be expressed. Sometimes it is important *not* to express how you feel for a variety of reasons. Let's discuss the nonexpression of emotions.

Emotions are very fleeting and often illogical. In other words, we can become emotional about something based on a lack of facts, our faulty perception of the facts, or our biological state at the moment.

Take this hypothetical situation for example: you have heard that a friend or colleague of yours made negative comments about you. You heard this from a third party who was not present when the comments were made. This third party heard the comments from someone who was present at the meeting. The normal reaction for most of us is to become angry.

The problem with becoming angry at this is, first of all, the "facts" you have come by may not be accurate due to being the product of second- and third-party hearsay. Second, sometimes the person who spread such information to you may have an ulterior motive. He or she may want to cause a problem between you and your colleague or friend, so he or she exaggerates the facts. Third, the friend or colleague may have said nothing about you, and if he or she did, what was said may have been taken out of context.

Another factor that can affect your reactions to the above scenario is the biological state you were in when you heard it. If the comment was made to you when you were already under stress about something else, it may accelerate your anger.

It is important that you consider how you process your emotions about the facts, perceptions of the facts, and your biological state before you express how you should feel. If you express how you feel based on faulty realities, you often cause harm.

Another reason not to express your emotions without hesitation is to consider the cost/benefit of doing so. When you express emotions, especially angry ones, the outcome for doing so may not be worth the price. If, for example, you express a negative emotion to someone who has authority over you such as your supervisor or a police officer who has stopped your vehicle, the consequences for doing so may worsen the situation. You have to be aware of how the other person might respond to receiving a flurry of negative emotions, especially if that person has formal authority over your actions.

On the other hand, many people in authority often feel they have the emotional authority to express how they feel no matter what. This can be sometimes construed as an abuse of authority. Unfortunately, when you have formal authority over someone, you may think you can get away with inappropriate emotional expression. This can come back to punish you, without you even knowing the source. When you abuse your authority through inappropriate emotional expression, the people you abuse may behave as if nothing is wrong. Still, they often have long memories and can be what scientists call passive-aggressive. They will find ways to retaliate, and you will not know it is those you abused in the first place.

A major issue with emotional expression is we often say one thing with our words, but our tone of voice and facial reactions say something totally different. This is because emotions are innately connected to our facial expressions and our voice tone.

For example, when we attempt to express an apology to someone for saying something out of anger, we may still convey that anger in our voice and face. This will happen if we still feel angry but are forced to apologize. Consequently, it is important to resolve how we really feel about something before we express our feelings.

It is also important to note that emotions can be contagious. Therefore if we express emotions toward others, those same emotions might be reciprocated. If you express negative emotions toward someone, there is a good chance you will receive negative emotions either directly or indirectly in return. Conversely if you express positive emotions toward someone, you will probably get positive emotions back.

The test at the end of this chapter is an assessment of your ability to express emotions constructively.

A person who has exemplified this dimension is Jackie Robinson.

Jackie Robinson—the first black professional baseball player

Jackie Robinson experienced a lot of discrimination and rejection, but due to his quiet emotional poise despite all this as well as his exceptional skills as a player, he was able to breach the racial gap for other black baseball players.

When Brooklyn Dodgers president Branch Rickey asked Jackie Robinson to join his team, he knew what challenges lay ahead for Robinson. When Robinson joined the major leagues in 1947, he was the first black man to play integrated baseball since the late 1890s.

Robinson endured harassment and ridicule from all directions, including his teammates. Other blacks certainly took pride in his achievements, because he was, after all, a magnificent player.

Fans shouted racial slurs at him, but nothing appeared to defeat Robinson's spirit. He quietly endured the discrimination and refused to express any

(continued)

disenchantment he may have felt. In doing so, he led the way for other black players to join the major leagues.

Robinson said, *"I'm not concerned with your liking or disliking me... All I ask is that you respect me as a human being."* (The Official Site of Jackie Robinson, n.d.)

Reception Ability

"Always forgive your enemies. Nothing annoys them so much."

– Oscar Wilde

Reception is the ability to manage others' emotions that are expressed directly or indirectly. This can be difficult because of the emotional contagion effect discussed above in the expression of emotions.

It appears that our ability to feel the emotions of others is the price we pay for being social animals. Our ability to work in groups has been critical to our survival versus other species. Our hunter-gatherer ancestors worked in groups when encountering animals that were much bigger and stronger than they were. By working in teams (strength in numbers), we were able to hunt and procure food.

It appears we have been preprogrammed, therefore, to sense the emotions of those around us as a means of survival. If someone who is near us senses fear, we may also become fearful—their fear alerts us to a threat.

Unfortunately this emotional connection between us and others has negative consequences also. If the persons around us become fearful, but the source of their fear is not based on facts, we can become fearful and act in harmful ways toward ourselves and others. This irrational group fear can create what is sometimes called a mob mentality or mass panic. Emotional receptivity can be a double-edged sword in our survival.

This receptivity can also be a problem when dealing with someone on a one-on-one basis. If someone becomes angry with you, the chances of you mirroring that anger increase significantly.

As a result, the ability not to let other persons' emotions affect us becomes crucial. For example, many domestic disputes between couples are the result of emotional receptivity. It appears this tendency to become emotional with loved ones is made worse because of our existing emotional closeness. Close feelings due to intimacy (loved ones and family) make it even more difficult to avoid being a victim of emotional receptivity, hence the saying, "We often hurt the ones we love."

Emotional receptivity can be positive, however, when it comes to human survival. Those emotions that make us charitable, loving, and forgiving are by-products of emotional receptivity. If you sense that a friend, loved one, or sometimes even a stranger is in pain, you may choose to help that person alleviate the suffering he or she may be going through.

We must be aware of both the negative and positive consequences of emotional receptivity. We have to know when to allow other people's feelings to affect us or not. For instance, it can be important not to convey anger at someone who is angry at you. If you become angry, the anger can escalate into something that is dangerous to both you and the other person. Road rage is often caused by this phenomenon. On the other hand, if someone conveys love or caring to you and you reciprocate that caring and love, it can result in a positive outcome.

A person who has exemplified this dimension is Tony Dungy.

Tony Dungy—former football coach, Indianapolis Colts

Tony Dungy is currently a commentator but was known for constant balanced displays of emotion on and off the field. When one of his sons committed suicide while at college, Dungy showed his pain with quiet resolve and sadness.

Dungy achieved success as a football coach in a manner very dissimilar from that of other coaches of his caliber. Dungy followed a simple coaching philosophy: he coached in a manner he himself would like to be coached.

Rather than screaming and provoking his players with threats, Dungy led by example. He associated the role of coach with that of a teacher. And even when things went wrong, he remained steadfastly calm ("Tony Dungy," n.d.).

Even when Dungy experienced the faith-rattling death of his son by suicide, Dungy grieved quietly and believed that somehow the tragedy was part of God's plan. Dungy said the choice to fight through the pain rather than succumb to it was necessary to move on.

"It's probably something I won't come to grips with," Dungy said of his son's death. *"But what it forces you to do is live in the present."*

Emotional Regulation Ability

> "I count him braver who overcomes his desires than him who conquers his enemies, the hardest victory is the victory over self."
>
> — Aristotle

Regulation is the ability to manage emotions that occur within us. It involves the awareness of our emotions as they occur and their impact on our thinking and actions. Emotions can occur so quickly within us that our ability to recognize, let alone manage, is a great source of difficulty.

Take for example post traumatic stress disorder (PTSD), which is common in soldiers, police officers, and others who experience traumatic life events. *Traumatic* comes from the word *trauma* meaning "wound." *Post* refers to the "past," and *stress* refers to emotional reactions. PTSD is therefore an emotional wound from a prior event. This event can take control of a person emotionally if he or she re-experiences aspects of the event. An anniversary date, a visual reminder, or even an odor associated with the initial event can trigger PTSD.

Every one of us can have forms of PTSD that are not as severe as clinically defined PTSD. Prior events in one's life that are sources of both emotional pain and pleasure can be re-enacted in the present emotionally. The intensity of these prior emotions is what causes the emotional memory of the brain to make them re-occur.

A key aspect of regulation is our ability to self-examine aspects of our emotional history that cause us problems in the present. For example, take an individual who had a very overbearing parent while growing up who attempted to micromanage everything that individual thought and did. This caused the individual to become emotionally over-wrought to the point that the individual vowed to never let anyone take control like that again. In the present, that individual works for a micro-managing boss. Some of the behaviors of the micro-managing boss remind that individual of his overbearing parent. At first the individual is able to regulate his emotions toward the micro-managing boss, but ultimately the individual's memories of his overbearing parent become too much and he lashes out at his boss, causing him to lose his job. This is the third job this person has lost due to his inability to deal with those in authority. At this point, the individual needs to assess the problem and its consequences.

Another factor to consider in emotional regulation is our biology. If we have low energy due to fatigue, hunger, or sleep deprivation, our ability to control our emotions is very difficult. Conversely, if we have high energy that has no outlet, emotions can be difficult to control. High energy people need activity. If that activity is stifled, it is hard to control emotions. Our biology, energy, and emotions are therefore intertwined.

For example, one of the definitions for *emotional depression* is "low energy to cope." The depression is caused by a lack of energy to cope with everyday activities that require a person to think and act. The depression is sometimes described as "numbing," meaning an inability to feel.

On the other hand, a person who has too much energy can become what is described as manic. *Manic* is a derivative of the word *mania*, which means "extreme enthusiasm to the point of mental abnormality." The person with this mental abnormality can become what is called a maniac. Maniacs have little emotional regulation ability; they feel indestructible and they are difficult to reason with.

A third aspect of regulation is prior learning about our emotions. Many of our emotional reactions are taught to us by prior learning. This prior learning often tells us how we *should* feel not necessarily *how* we feel.

For example, telling a youth league football player whose tendency is not to be aggressive, to be aggressive if he wants to continue playing can reverse his emotional predisposition to not be aggressive. Conversely, telling a young person not to become aggressive when he or she is being bullied by another child can reverse his or her predisposition.

Learning how we are supposed to feel about life events can be taught directly and indirectly. A child watching a parent become angry at a driver in another car can tell that child becoming angry is how he or she is supposed to feel. A lot of our learning is derived from imitation of what we see others do and feel.

A fourth factor in regulation ability is the way we perceive or think about life events. The way we evaluate events has a lot to do with how we feel about those events. If you are taught to view people who are homeless as irresponsible and lazy, then you will probably feel disdain toward them. On the other hand, if you view homeless people as victims of poor upbringing or unfortunate circumstances, you may feel empathy or compassion instead.

The way you think can affect your ability to regulate how you feel. It was mentioned earlier in this chapter that how you feel can affect the way you think. Both these statements are true. The key to regulating how you feel when it is caused by the way you think is to change the way you think. This can be done by trying to think in ways that are not the norm for you.

For example, if you were to think (believe) that you were not successful financially as you would have liked, you may feel unhappy with yourself. You then begin to think about your financially successful friend whose child has a terminal illness. You realize that your children are all healthy and thriving. You may start to rethink that financial success is not as important as the health and well-being of your loved ones. You may then begin to feel that not being happy about your lack of financial success needs to change due to your personal success of healthy children.

A fifth factor in emotional regulation is your ability to attribute your emotional state on something other than external factors, namely yourself. Many people believe their negative emotions are caused by other people or events in their life. They are willing to believe that they are not responsible for how they feel. They have a sense that they are emotionally entitled to blame other circumstances rather than take personal responsibility.

You will often hear people say, "You made me feel that way" or "If you hadn't said that or done that, I wouldn't have gotten angry." If you believe that you are not ultimately responsible for most of your feelings, you are conceding to a state of emotional powerlessness.

One of the ways to counter this emotional powerlessness is to ask yourself, "Why am I letting this get to me?" or tell yourself "I'm feeling angry with myself for letting this bother me." This is the first step to gaining control. It is basically taking responsibility about how you feel and not blaming it on or externalizing the cause on to outside forces. You are ultimately responsible for how you choose to feel, as difficult as that may be.

A person who has exemplified this dimension is James B. Stockdale.

James B. Stockdale, Admiral—Medal of Honor recipient

Admiral James B. Stockdale was shot down over North Vietnam in 1965 and spent seven years in captivity. Throughout his captivity and the attempts to break his spirit, he refused to cooperate with his captors despite being tortured 15 times.

Admiral Stockdale was the highest-ranking serviceman ever to be captured and held as a POW. For seven years, Stockdale endured unrelenting torture and psychological abuse from his North Vietnamese captors.

Despite regular beatings and long periods of solitary confinement, Stockdale never lost hope that he and his men would be released. *"I never lost faith in the end of the story, I never doubted that not only would I get out but also that I would prevail in the end and turn the experience into the defining moment of my life, which, in retrospect, I would not trade."*

During their captivity, Stockdale and other American POWs used ingenuity and willpower to survive. They created a code by which they could communicate. Near the pinnacle of this period of captivity, Stockdale inflicted serious, life-threatening wounds upon himself to signal to the North Vietnamese that they could never succeed in breaking him. Eventually their treatment of the POWs improved, and Stockdale was released in early 1973 ("James Stockdale Biography—Academy of Achievement," 2010).

Emotionality Test

Let's measure your emotionality potential.

Below are some questions and actions that measure your emotionality skills. Answer the questions and rate the statements honestly. Use the following scale and place a check (✓) in the box to rate yourself for each question or statement.

1 = Rarely   2 = Sometimes   3 = Usually   4 = Often   5 = A Lot

You may want to ask some people who know you well to rate you, using the same scale. See how closely your score and their scores match. Don't be surprised if there is a big difference.

	1	2	3	4	5
1. How often do you ask yourself "What am I feeling at this moment?"	❏	❏	❏	❏	❏
2. When talking on the phone with someone, do you pay conscious attention to their tone of voice?	❏	❏	❏	❏	❏
3. Do you pay close attention to how your moods (angry, anxious, sad, happy) affect your thinking?	❏	❏	❏	❏	❏
4. You try to be aware of your facial expression when expressing feelings toward someone else.	❏	❏	❏	❏	❏
5. You take the time to consider what has made you angry before expressing it.	❏	❏	❏	❏	❏
6. You tell people who are close to you (family/friends) that you care about them.	❏	❏	❏	❏	❏
7. You try to determine the reasons for a person's feelings before reacting to them.	❏	❏	❏	❏	❏
8. You listen carefully to a person's tone of voice to determine what they are feeling.	❏	❏	❏	❏	❏

	1	2	3	4	5
9. You ask yourself when someone has offended you "Why do I feel offended right now?"	❏	❏	❏	❏	❏
10. You pay attention to how you act toward others when you are feeling tired and/or fatigued.	❏	❏	❏	❏	❏

Scoring:

Add your total score and multiply the total by 2. This number is your ability potential in this dimension. For example: 30 × 2 = 60% ability in this range.

A score above 80% is a good score.

A score above 90% is an excellent score.

Note: A more accurate assessment of your ability in this dimension, which consists of 40 statements/questions versus the 10 shown in this book, can be found at www.sotelligence.com.

References

Cacioppo, J. T., & Patrick, W. (2008). *Loneliness: Human nature and the need for social connection*. New York: W.W. Norton & Company.

Dunning, D. (2005). *Self-insights: Roadblocks and detours on the path to knowing thyself*. New York: Psychology Press.

Dunstan Baby (Director). (2006). *Dunstan baby language* [Motion picture on DVD]. U.S.

Ekman, P. (2003). *Emotions revealed: Recognizing faces and feelings to improve communication and emotional life*. New York: Henry Holt.

Ekman, P., & Friesen, W. V. (2003). *Unmasking the face: A guide to recognizing emotions from facial clues*. Cambridge, MA: Malor Books.

Goleman, D. (1995). *Emotional intelligence*. New York: Bantam Books.

Gottman, J. M. (2005). *The mathematics of marriage: Dynamic nonlinear models*. Cambridge, MA: MIT Press.

James Stockdale Biography—Academy of Achievement. (2010, June 17). *Academy of Achievement Main Menu*. Retrieved December 18, 2010, from http://www.achievement.org/autodoc/page/sto0bio-1

LeDoux, J. E. (1996). *The emotional brain*. New York: Simon and Schuster.

Mehrabian, A. (1971). *Silent messages* (1st ed.). Belmont, CA: Wadsworth.

Neumarkt, P. (2005). The dimension of psychology. *The Journal of Evolutionary Psychology, 26*.

Norman Schwarzkopf Interview—Academy of Achievement. (2007, December 14). *Academy of Achievement Main Menu*. Retrieved December 18, 2010, from http://www.achievement.org/autodoc/page/sch0int-1

Seligman, M. E. (2002). *Authentic happiness: Using the new positive psychology to realize your potential for lasting fulfillment.* New York: Free Press.

Shermer, M. (2005). *The science of good and evil: Why people cheat, gossip, care, share, and follow the Golden Rule.* New York: H. Holt and Co.

The Official Site of Jackie Robinson. (n.d.). Retrieved December 18, 2010, from http://www.jackierobinson.com/about/bio.html

Tomkins, S., Demos, E., & Smith, B. (1995). *Exploring affect.* Cambridge University Press. Cambridge Books Online. Cambridge University Press. 01 January 2011 http://dx.doi.org/10.1017/CBO9780511663994.005

Tony Dungy. (n.d.). *Wikipedia, the free encyclopedia.* Retrieved December 17, 2010, from http://en.wikipedia.org/wiki/Tony_Dungy

Westen, D. (2007). *The political brain: The role of emotion in deciding the fate of the nation.* New York: Public Affairs.

Chapter 6

Personability Dimension

> "There are three things extremely hard: steel, a diamond, and to know oneself."
>
> – Benjamin Franklin

This is an area of self-development that is relatively new in terms of scientific study. Personability is the ability to personalize or to take personally what occurs around us. The phrase *know thyself* is synonymous with personability, and *self-aware* is a term that some scientists currently use. The term *intrapersonal* is frequently used in the social science literature to describe this ability to communicate with oneself, whereas interpersonability refers to one's ability to communicate with others.

The goal of personability is self-improvement through self-awareness. That is probably why public speaking is consistently judged as the greatest cause of anxiety in people. Public speaking makes a person totally visible to numerous people and therefore makes the person susceptible to harsh judgments if the person was to make errors or fail.

As human beings, we share the inclination to justify ourselves when we are wrong and avoid responsibility for actions that are harmful, immoral, and stupid. It is also in our nature to take credit when things go right and blame others when things go wrong.

Unfortunately, this self-blindness is often destructive to both ourselves and others. For example, John Gottman and his colleagues observed married couples interacting for 15 minutes and measured the emotion in the couples' tones of voice and facial expressions. Once Gottman and his researchers analyzed the data (emotional patterns), they were able to predict marital success or failure (divorce). The couples, however, were unable to see or hear these micro-vocal and facial expressions that were affecting their marriages (Carrere & Gottman, 1999).

At the Oracle of Delphi was the admonition: "Know Thyself." David Dunning's book *Self-Insight* discusses the extent to which a person knows him- or herself. The premise of the book was that people need to know their strengths and weaknesses and their moral character so when faced with temptation, they might not commit sins they will later regret or be punished for (2005).

William James, who many consider the father of American psychology, discussed the issue of self in his 1890 book *The Principles of Psychology*. One of James's major contentions was that although we might feel like a "unique" entity (i.e., my name is John and this is who I am), a person has many facets, from awareness of one's own body, thoughts, feelings, to memories of oneself, to how one fits in society. James professed that he was stumped as to how the brain took all these facets of who a person is and then wove them into a single human being.

David Dunning, probably one of the most cited scientists in the area of current self-insight research, states that individuals' ability to accurately self-rate their own skills and actual performances in many domains is moderate to meager, which suggests that people overrate themselves. He also suggests that other people's perceptions of our abilities and performances prove more accurate than a person's self-predictions (Dunning, Heath, & Suls, 2004).

A major area in animal intelligence research is determining an animal's ability to first see itself in a mirror and realize it is looking at *itself* as opposed to another animal (realization of self). Many scientists believe an animal's ability to realize it is seeing itself is an indicator of its intelligence as a species. Because a chimpanzee has the ability to recognize itself and a cat does not, it can be assumed that the chimpanzee has a greater level of intelligence than the cat.

Let us examine some of the facts about personability in humans.

Fact 1: Self-deception may be more self-destructive than deception toward others.

Lying to oneself is a common occurrence. Sometimes we do it by rationalizing our actions even though our gut reactions make us question it. We often do this when we have to make decisions that may benefit others instead of ourselves, and consequently we often make the decision that benefits our needs first. This type of self-deception is often associated with criminal acts.

On the other hand, we may lie to ourselves to justify a course of action we have undertaken that is obviously failing us. We do this when we cling to unprofitable investments, businesses that are failing, the "lemon" car we purchased, or the business deal that turns out to be too good to be true.

We often lie to ourselves when we overinflate our abilities. The health-care practice of playing one's own doctor demonstrates the serious consequences. For example, some people believe they are invulnerable to the flu and avoid flu shots. Then there are others who think they are less likely than someone else to acquire sexually transmitted diseases and are then more likely to engage in high-risk sex acts. Some people with high blood pressure believe they can self-monitor their blood pressure and only take the medicine when they think they need it rather than how it is prescribed (Martin & Leventhal, 2004). Such behaviors can lead to serious medical problems and even death.

Fact 2: A little knowledge may be just as dangerous to our self-insight as none at all.

The way we learn in today's world may give a false sense of our abilities. Students tend to be overly self-assured about their newly learned abilities given some teaching methods. David Dunning and his team suggest that the current system of massed learning (learning material over a long period of time) can promote rapid acquisition of skill and self-confidence but not the retention of knowledge and skill (Dunning, Heath, & Suls, 2004).

Dunning, et al., report this is typical of driver education courses that do not produce safe drivers. If the training was spaced and distributed over time, the students would learn more slowly and therefore retain more.

Some researchers have reported that certain forms of driver education can actually cause more harm because they give the new driver an inflated sense of confidence that only long-term learning can address. This type of approach can cause "overconfidence training" that does not address adverse driving situations such as poor weather, vehicle mechanical problems, or dangerous traffic conditions.

Fact 3: Faulty memories of what happened in prior personal failures may cause us to be more forgiving of ourselves.

Carol Tavris and Eliot Aronson's book *Mistakes Were Made (But Not by Me)*, presents the idea that memory is a self-justifying historian as previously discussed. The authors propose that human beings as story tellers have a tendency to spin a story to make themselves look better. They tend to incorrectly remember what they did wrong to cause prior failures (Tavris & Aronson, 2007).

Tavris and Aronson discuss the case of Binjamin Wilkomirski who published a memoir describing "his" experiences in a concentration camp. Wilkomirski's real name was Bruno Grosjean; he was not Jewish, and he had never been in a concentration camp (Dunning, Heath, & Suls, 2004). In fact, Wilkomirski was raised in an orphanage. He was abandoned by his single mother and was later adopted but had very little recollection of his first four years of life.

Wilkomirski began to obsess about his early life and began reading about the Holocaust and identifying with the Jews. He had visited Majdanek (a concentration camp), and subsequently "falsely" remembered he had been there as a young boy. While in psychotherapy, he was told to write down his memories of the concentration camp (Dunning, Heath, & Suls, 2004). Obviously in trying to remember something that never happened, he quickly injected fiction to support his belief.

It is important to keep in mind some facts about memories. No one wants to believe a vivid memory is wrong regardless of what others think. Also, simply because someone has convinced himself that a memory is true does not make it so. Finally, memory errors are frequently used to support our feelings and beliefs about our past.

Fact 4: When we experience mental conflict, we will justify our mistakes to lower the stress of mental conflict.

Leon Festinger spent much of his career as a psychologist/researcher studying what he called *cognitive dissonance.* He described it as a state of tension that occurs when someone holds two cognitions (ideas, beliefs, or opinions) that are in conflict with each other (Festinger, 1957).

For example, if someone has a strong belief that his closest friend would never betray him, but is given indisputable facts that the friend has, the mental conflict it would cause could be unbearable. In order to deal with this mental discomfort, the person may convince himself that the indisputable facts are obviously wrong and continue to trust the friend anyway.

Another variable strongly associated with cognitive dissonance is confirmation bias. We have a natural tendency to confirm information that supports our beliefs and expectations and disconfirm facts that do not.

A study on the effectiveness of the death penalty demonstrates how confirmation works. Students were asked to review two research studies—one that confirmed the effectiveness of the death penalty and another that did not. The students were asked before reviewing the studies their position on the effectiveness of the death penalty. It turned out that if the study supported the students' position, they thought the study was well conducted. Conversely, if the study results did not confirm their bias, they found numerous flaws in the study that discounted its validity (Lord, Ross, & Lepper, 1979).

This confirmation bias can have disastrous results in a leadership situation. In 1941, Admiral Kimmel was Pacific Fleet Commander. He had been repeatedly warned of the possible war with the Japanese, but the admiral did not believe the United States was in any danger. On December 3, he received intelligence that the Japanese had ordered their embassies to destroy most of their codes. Kimmel took the position that "most" did not mean "all." Approximately one hour before the attack on Pearl Harbor, a Japanese submarine was sunk near the entry to Pearl Harbor. The admiral did not respond to that, and consequently, the Pacific Fleet was totally vulnerable. The fleet was destroyed and Kimmel was court-martialed. Admiral Kimmel could not change the way he thought about the Japanese attacking the United States despite facts that disconfirmed his beliefs (Sutherland, 1994).

This phenomenon is very prevalent in gambling. Many gamblers rationalize their losses by rewriting their successes against their failures in their mind. Sometimes gamblers evaluate their losses as near wins (Gilovich, 1983).

Our inability to deal with the mental conflict of information that disconfirms our beliefs contributes to our inability to see our flaws.

Fact 5: The average person frequently claims to be above average.

Dunning's book *Self-Insight: Roadblocks and Detours on the Path to Knowing Thyself* discusses how people frequently overestimate their abilities. For example, a person's notion about his or her performance on an intelligence test correlates only 0.2 to 0.3 with actual performance. This means there is between a 10 percent to 15 percent chance their perceptions are accurate and an 85 percent to 90 percent chance they are inaccurate (Dunning, 2005).

According to Dunning, when it comes to complex social interaction competence, the correlation between how people are perceived by others compared to what they think of themselves is a 0.17 correlation on average (Dunning, 2005). This implies that there is a 91.5 percent chance their social interactions and social perceptions are incorrect.

Overestimating abilities is not limited to IQ test performance. In a 1976–77 College Board survey of nearly one million high school seniors, 70 percent claimed they had above-average leadership skills, and 60 percent of these same students gave themselves high marks for getting along with others (Alicke & Govorun, 2005).

Even professionals overestimate their abilities. In Jay Christensen-Szalanski's 1981 study at the University of Iowa, he found that physicians believed they correctly diagnosed pneumonia in 88 percent of cases when in reality they only made correct diagnoses in 20 percent of them (Christensen-Szalanski & Bushyhead, 1981).

Some people are better at estimating their abilities given the nature of their activities. For athletes where an athlete's performance is often measured in statistics, such as a baseball player's batting average, the correlations typically run around 0.47. Athletes also receive constant feedback from coaches as to their performances, which increases their self-judgment accuracy.

There are several other examples of this overconfidence in one's ability from a variety of scientific studies. College students are better at predicting the longevity of their roommates' romantic relationships than the roommates themselves (MacDonald & Ross, 1999).

A survey of lawyers conducted by Loftus and Wagenaar (1988) found that lawyers overestimated the likelihood they would win cases they were about to try.

These same people who view themselves as above average in many domains believe they personally do not overestimate their abilities but believe others do. In a study conducted by Pronin, et al. (2002), when people were asked directly about their overconfidence, they reported the following: they tended to say that they were uniquely able to avoid overconfidence and bias that other people could not.

Fact 6: The ambiguity of words and concepts that describe human traits can shield us from how we really behave.

P. W. Bridgeman, a Nobel-Prize–winning physicist, said the validity of a scientific term does not lie in the words that define it but in the actions it represents.

Traits like intelligence, leadership, maturity, and integrity are difficult to define in behavioral or actionable terms. Dunning utilizes a term called *trait ambiguity*. For example, in looking at the trait of dominance, those who see themselves as dominant describe it as a good trait. Those who do not consider themselves dominant perceive dominance differently, meaning that dominant people monopolize conversations and order people around.

Trait ambiguity, according to Dunning, has a self-serving tendency. Sometimes people adapt definitions of traits that emphasize something they are naturally good at such as math. For such individuals, the degree to which a person is good at math must be a measure of the person's overall intelligence (Dunning, 2005).

People create these self-serving trait definitions to maintain their sense of self-worth. Take the example of Joe Henson, who is the new police chief of a relatively large metropolitan police department. He describes himself as a strong, no-nonsense, results-driven leader. He states that he holds weekly meetings with his zone commanders on the number of arrests each zone is making for various crimes. He tells the zone commanders he expects the crime statistics to reflect a decline in crime, or he will find someone else who can do the job. When Chief Henson's zone commanders are asked to describe their leader, they say he is autocratic and unwilling to take suggestions about his unrealistic expectations regarding crime control.

Eventually, the reported crime statistic reductions in Chief Henson's city are so incredible that a newspaper story comes out on the national news. Eventually, a well-known criminologist looking at Chief Henson's reported crime reductions says they are statistically impossible to achieve. An investigative reporter with the local newspaper in Chief Henson's town initiates an inquiry. The reporter eventually finds out that some of the zone commanders had intentionally under-reported crime rates in the city to avoid losing their positions.

In this instance, Chief Henson's trait ambiguity description as a strong, no-nonsense, results-driven leader was perceived by his subordinates as autocratic and unrealistic. Chief Henson's self-perception led him to believe the crime reduction rates were the results of his strong leadership, when in reality they led to his downfall.

Fact 7: Power and status can increase the probability of false sense of self.

The chapter entitled "The Ethnic Theory of Plane Crashes" in Malcolm Gladwell's book *Outliers* (2008) discusses how power and status can insulate those in power from their flaws. The chapter reviews the significant number of plane crashes experienced by Korean Air Lines compared with other airlines in the 1990s. It appears that after examining the possible causes of these crashes, none of the crashes were due to faulty plane equipment. All the crashes were due to pilot error. The investigations into crashes concluded that the crashes were due to what is called "high power distance" ethic among the crew members in the cockpit just prior to the crashes.

A Dutch researcher named Geert Hofstede (as cited in Gladwell, 2008) coined the term *high power distance* versus *low power distance* when describing how cultures differ around the world in their approaches to managing those in authority in their cultures. The term *high power distance* refers to the view that in high power distance cultures, those in authority are never questioned by subordinates. To question authority is highly inappropriate (Gladwell, 2008).

Based on a review of the black box recordings in these Korean Air Lines crashes, the cockpit's crew members attempted to gently forewarn their captains that a crash was imminent unless they changed course. It appears that the airliner captain ignored these suggestions since subordinates should never question his authority (Gladwell, 2008).

It also appears that not only power itself, but one's social status can insulate such individuals from self-critique or criticism from others. This is very common when someone is a celebrity such as a professional actor, athlete, or politician. Unfortunately, the public often assumes that celebrities and high-status individuals are unflawed because they could not have achieved stardom or status if they were flawed to begin with.

- O. J. Simpson, the famous football player, was charged with the murder of his former wife and her friend. Simpson was seen by many as not capable of this crime because of his reputation as a well-known athlete. His public image prior to the charge was that of a nice guy.

- The multitude of accusations against Catholic priests as having molested young male and female members of their Church shocked the American public. This issue was exacerbated by the Church's apparent initial attempt to avoid responsibility for these occurrences. Prior to this, Catholic priests were revered.

- President Richard Nixon's fall from grace after the revelations surrounding Watergate is a classic example of a politician who was previously well-respected given his foreign policy skills. Later, people were shocked at the amount of profanity he used on a regular basis on the infamous White House tape recordings of his office conversations.

Fact 8: We tend to justify our actions that are frequently wrong when going up against adversaries.

In many conflicts between individuals and groups, each side often justifies their position by claiming the other is to blame. This is true in conflicts between friends, family members, and even countries when they disagree about who started what and when.

In Carol Tavris's book *Mistakes Were Made (But Not by Me)* she discusses the varying perceptions of perpetrators and victims. Perpetrators of injuries are motivated to reduce their moral responsibility, and victims try to enhance their moral blamelessness (Tavris & Aronson, 2007). She states the perpetrators usually report that what they did was reasonable, and though they might regret what happened, it was understandable given the situation they were in. Some even blame the victim, saying the victim precipitated their victimization. Even when perpetrators admit they are wrong, they try to forget about it as quickly as possible (Tavris & Aronson, 2007).

In a road rage situation, for example, the driver who becomes angry due to the indiscretion of another driver will say he or she became angry because the other person almost caused him or her to have an accident. These individuals often believe their anger and subsequent road rage were acceptable given the threat they felt.

This author remembers an incident when stopped at a traffic light behind two vehicles. I saw the male driver of the car in front of me exit his vehicle. He approached the first car with what appeared to be a cup of hot coffee in his hands. He tapped the window of this vehicle. When the driver, a female, lowered the window, he threw the hot coffee in her face. I decided to exit my vehicle to see why this occurred. I called out to the male driver who threw the coffee and asked if everything was alright. He responded that the woman had cut him off about a mile back. When I started to call 911 on my cell phone, he asked what I was doing. I told him I was calling the police. He looked at me and asked why. I told him he assaulted the woman. He looked stunned and proceeded to go to his vehicle. I told him I had memorized his license plate number. Several other people began to exit their vehicles behind me. They showed their disdain for the male driver's actions when they realized what had occurred. When the police arrived, the male driver began to justify his actions as a perpetrator.

Tavris also points out that many perpetrators actually perceive themselves as victims and therefore justify their retribution. Their victimization absolves them of responsibility (Tavris & Aronson, 2007).

In the above scenario involving the thrown coffee, the male driver proceeded to tell the police officer he threw the coffee in the woman's face because the woman nearly caused him to have a wreck. It appears this coffee-throwing driver perceived he was the victim and that justified his subsequent actions.

This type of self-justification is also common in marriages and is often a major contributor to marriages ending. Couples in marital distress often blame their partners as to why the divorce occurred. Gottman's groundbreaking research on divorce prediction finds the more adversarial a couple is or one partner becomes, the greater the chance for divorce. Gottman states that as a couple begins to feel contemptuous and adversarial, they develop their own theories of how the other person is wrecking the marriage. They actually begin to rewrite their memory of why the relationship went bad to justify their negative actions, and ultimately they begin to justify name calling, criticism, screaming at each other, and even physical attack. They believe they are victims and therefore are allowed to be perpetrators (Gottman & Silver, 1994).

Fact 9: Smart people often do dumb things, which often indicates a lack of self-awareness regarding practical intelligence.

Robert K. Wagner, the author of many articles on intelligence, discusses the lack of "tacit intelligence or knowledge" as a phenomenon that contributes to obviously intelligent people doing dumb things. Tacit knowledge is an awareness of practical problems and their solutions based on experience as opposed to "book" knowledge. It is also an ability to solve problems when there is no single correct answer because there is a lack of essential information to solve them.

In a book entitled, *Why Smart People Can Be So Stupid*, edited by Robert Sternberg, Wagner (2003) discusses the major successes and yet ultimate failure of the president of a large major university. Below is his description of the rise and fall of this university president.

> A provost's term at a major private university was marked by unprecedented success. Eagerly sought by search committees, he accepted an offer to be president of a large state university. By all objective indicators, his success continued. During his presidency, huge increases were achieved in the university's endowment and amount of funded research. Undergraduate enrollment increased, as did the average SAT scores of admitted students. Ranking of program quality by the National Research Council indicated improvement in already high-quality programs for the most part. Yet recently this president resigned under pressure.
>
> When I mentioned this situation to a colleague from a private university in the Midwest, he categorized it as yet another example of a successful administrator from a northern private university falling victim to the politics of a public university system in a southern state.
>
> There may be a bit of truth in his characterization. The president's first public brush with trouble came several years ago, when he was chastised publicly by the chancellor and board of regents for working unilaterally with the state legislature to benefit his university. University presidents are supposed to work exclusively through the board of regents, which represents the entire state university system to the legislature. Although all public institutions in the state are supposed to present proposals to the board of regents, which then negotiates with the legislature, it is no secret that the top administrators of larger schools work hard to cultivate relationships with individual members of the legislature who may be inclined to be helpful. If anything, the president's early trouble arose because he was so successful in working with the legislature

for the benefit of his university that he upstaged the chancellor, an individual with no small ego. He rode out the rift with the chancellor successfully, aided by politically powerful backers. Things even began to look rosy when the chancellor accepted a job elsewhere.

The president, a scholar and administrator known for his remarkable intellect, then made several apparent missteps that eventually led to his resignation. First, according to press reports, he used a pejorative term to describe an incoming chancellor in a private conversation at a holiday party for members of his administration. The remark was leaked to the press. Next, news reports indicate that two visiting deans who reviewed part of the university complained to the chancellor and school officials that the president acted like an arrogant, abusive bully in their interactions with him. Then, three weeks before agreeing to resign, the president was reported to have given substantial raises to top administrators without seeking the approval of the chancellor.

The above is an example that self-awareness of what you do know may not be enough to manage the uniqueness of the reality you are in. The university president in the above example lacked the unique tacit/practical knowledge necessary to be successful in the context he was in. As president, he assumed his earned intellectual ability was sufficient to be successful. His inability to reflect his current intellectual ability was not sufficient and led to his downfall.

The constant questioning of what you do know and the constant pursuit of new knowledge and skills that embrace both formal learning and informal learning can mitigate being smart yet stupid.

Fact 10: A paradox exists between overconfidence and no confidence.

A paradox is defined as a seemingly absurd or contradictory statement even if actually well-founded. Overconfidence may be dangerous to our self-insight, but a lack of confidence in oneself and the accompanying questioning of oneself can also be. The power of confidence and psychological well-being and the accompanying willingness to take chances is obviously related to self-development. On the other hand, over-confidence, often due to blind self-awareness, can be self-destructive and destructive to others. Dunning's book on self-insight, mentioned earlier in this chapter, discusses the fact that people who have confidence in their abilities persevere in the face of challenges, and this often leads to better performance (2005).

- Studies have shown that people who are trying to lose weight succeed to the extent they believe they can.

- Children who believe in their mathematical abilities work longer on math problems.

- There are numerous stories of successful entrepreneurs who were initially faced with constant failure and setbacks, but their belief in themselves helped them persevere.

Ted Turner, the notorious "Mouth of the South," who developed CNN and other mass media enterprises, experienced several setbacks in both his personal and professional lives. Turner was known for verbal irreverence and hypo-manic tendencies. He was eventually diagnosed with manic-depression later in his life and self-reported that psychiatric medication turned his life around. Overconfidence and the diagnosis of mania are closely associated. One of the major symptoms of mania is grandiosity of beliefs and actions. Basically when people become manic, their overconfidence becomes too ambitious and not realistically attainable.

Dunning addresses the above issue by stressing how the pros and cons of overconfidence can be reconciled. He states that addressing the cost and benefits realistically is the key. The benefit is the degree to which a goal is realistically achievable considering the cost it would take to achieve it (Dunning, 2005).

An example would be an individual going back to school to earn a medical degree while married with children and then managing the accompanying financial distress it could bring. In achieving the medical degree, the person's responsibilities to his or her family may become minimized to the point of divorce and estrangement from one's family. The divorce and estrangement from family may not be worth the cost.

The quote by Louisa May Alcott addresses the paradox of confidence and no confidence:

> Conceit spoils the finest genius. There is not much danger that real talent or goodness will overlook for long; even if it is, the consciousness of possessing and using it well should satisfy, and the great charm of all power is modesty.

Developing and Applying Your Personability

Openness

> "No one ever understands quite their own artful dodges to escape from the grim shadow of self-knowledge."
>
> – Joseph Conrad

The study of personality and how to measure it in people has been ongoing in psychology for over 60 years. In the 1970s, two research teams, one from the National Institute of Health and the other from the University of Michigan, discovered that most human traits can be described using five dimensions (McRae & John, 1992). These five dimensions are *openness*, *agreeableness*, *conscientiousness*, *extroversion*, and *neuroticism.*

One of these "big five," openness, is critical to self-awareness. Openness is defined as a personality trait that seeks novelty and likes to be creative. People low in the openness subdimension are described as more conventional in their thinking, prefer routines, and have a pronounced sense of right and wrong.

The German philosopher Count Hermann von Keyserling stated the shortest path to oneself is around the world. Keyserling believed that travel was the best way to discover who one is. When traveling to other cultures, individuals encounter novel and unfamiliar experiences that force them to constantly adjust how they think, feel, and act. Changing thoughts, feelings, and actions requires going beyond one's comfort level, and this requires openness to change.

One does not have to travel to experience openness. When people pursue formal education to better themselves, they are often forced to be open to new ideas and knowledge. This is especially true when they have to learn about subjects they may not be otherwise interested in.

Individuals also have to be open when they have to encounter people outside their own social group or social comfort zone. This is especially true when we participate in the practices of other cultures and social groups. This could be done by attending a church that is not the practitioner of our own religious beliefs or by experiencing the foods of a culture outside our own.

The key to openness is the desire to seek novelty or newness that goes against the habits and values one is comfortable with. Openness does not require having to accept all novel experiences in a positive way; many novel experiences can affect us in a negative way. These negative experiences can tell us a lot about ourselves.

For example, trying out for a sports team in school and failing to make it can be painful but self-educational. The failure may reveal that the person is not talented enough to perform. The person can therefore accept that this was not meant for him or her. This type of failure further makes the person aware of his or her limitations.

On the other hand, the above failure may motivate the person to acquire new skills and knowledge through hard work and practice. If the person eventually succeeds and makes the team, it teaches him or her that abilities that do not come easily take more effort to acquire.

Openness typically increases during a person's 20s and goes into a gradual decline. Many theorists believe personality traits change during young adulthood, despite the influence of genetics on our personality. The reason may be that young adulthood is a time where many life changes occur in terms of developing a career, finding a spouse or partner, and starting families.

It appears that people continue to change somewhat in middle and old age, but openness to new experience tends to diminish until about 60 years old. It appears that after 60, some people become open again because many of their day-to-day obligations (raising a family and earning a living) are not there (Srivastava, et al., 2003).

A person who has exemplified this dimension is Herschel Walker.

Herschel Walker—College and Professional Football Player

Herschel Walker once said, "As long as you are trying to beat the other guy over there and you are worried about him, you are not worrying about how you got to perform." He started out as an unathletic child, but became one of the greatest players in college football history. He recently stated publicly that he had a major psychological problem he was now addressing.

When Herschel Walker was young, he did not seem to possess any inclination to participate in sports. In fact, he has said many times that he was "unathletic." When Walker determined he could be "cool" if he participated in sports, he began a training regimen. He was also motivated to perform well in academics.

His seemingly simple belief that he could succeed in both academics and athletics if he pushed himself hard enough yielded great rewards. He was valedictorian of his high school class and was one of the most sought-after high school football players in 1980.

At the University of Georgia, he set a rushing record as a freshman, and eventually became an All-American and Heisman Trophy winner. The Collegiate Football Hall of Fame rated him as one of the greatest football players of all time, just behind Red Grange. Eventually, Walker turned pro.

"Mistakes should be taken as a training tool to help you get better," Walker said. Even though Walker apparently did not make many mistakes throughout his life, he recently revealed that he has struggled with mental illness but has been receiving treatment. In making his affliction public, Walker hopes to help others and create understanding about his disorder. ("Herschel Walker Biography—Academy of Achievement," 2010).

Insight

> "The person with insight enough to admit his/her limitations comes nearest to perfection."
>
> – Johann von Geotne

The ability to have insight refers to seeing inside ourselves rather than looking outside ourselves. When we are looking at a star, a tree, or a person, we are viewing things outside ourselves. When we are thinking about the type of facial expression we are displaying or hand gestures we are exhibiting, we are looking at ourselves.

The term *insight* does not just refer to literally seeing inside ourselves. It refers to our ability to be internally aware of other states occurring inside of ourselves. This includes what I am thinking at this moment, what I am feeling at this moment, and what I am saying at this moment. All too often we are not closely monitoring our actions, thoughts, feelings, or words.

Some scientists refer to self-insight as self-monitoring ability. We often act, think, feel, or verbalize outside any conscious sense of it. This is due to our tendency to be creatures of habit. Habits are learned actions, thoughts, feelings, or words that are so programmed into us that they occur without self-insight. We tend to like habits because we do not have to think and feel the discomfort of inhabiting ourselves. Self-insight is therefore difficult to achieve because it requires going against habits; sometimes this is referred to as self-discipline.

The power of insight is ultimately self-control and therefore more control over what is happening to us. We have all had experiences where we wish we could take back something we said or did because the consequences we experienced were painful for us. If we were closely monitoring our actions, thoughts, emotions, and words, these negative consequences would occur less frequently in our lives.

For example, not paying close attention to our emotions and their effect on our facial expressions and voice tone often has social consequences in our relationships. If someone is in a negative emotional state as he or she arrives home and is hoping for a peaceful evening, he or she may just get the opposite if he or she cannot hide it.

A person who has exemplified this dimension is John Wooden.

John Wooden—College Basketball Coach

John Wooden was beloved by his players because of his attention to detail and the way he constantly required his players to self-monitor their actions on and off the court. Wooden was also known for his self-monitoring in that he never used profanity.

John Wooden credits his humble life on his family's farm with giving him the drive to succeed later. Despite his success as a Purdue University basketball player (he was an All-American), Wooden chose to become an English teacher rather than become a professional basketball player. (He wanted to marry his high school sweetheart.)

He began coaching high school basketball and eventually coached college basketball. Wooden left Indiana to coach the UCLA Bruins in 1948 and took one of the weakest teams in their division and made them the best.

Wooden's coaching style revolved around showing genuine love and concern for his players. He refrained from using a dictatorial style, never used profanity, and refused to allow his players to use it as well.

In this way, Wooden was a master of self-monitoring. And as a coach, he is one of the most successful. In his 27 years coaching the Bruins, they did not have a losing season. In fact, they won 10 National Championships.

Wooden saw potential in everyone he met: *"We are all absolutely equal in having the opportunity to make the most of what we have."* ("John Wooden Biography—Academy of Achievement," 2010).

Ownership

> "We run away all the time to avoid coming face to face with ourselves."
>
> – Anonymous

Ownership is the ability to take blame/responsibility for our negative actions, feelings, and thoughts. It is one of the most difficult things to do for most of us. This is because it affects our self-esteem, is painful, and is often so fatiguing it feels like the "wind has literally been knocked out of us." It is in our innate nature to self-protect, and it is also in our nature to fend for ourselves in a world that often requires competition and survival of the fittest.

When we take ownership, we have to view ourselves as possibly weak, fallible, and therefore vulnerable. When we are vulnerable, we can be susceptible to being taken advantage of. Taking ownership can also weaken us in terms of questioning our ability to cope with life in general.

A common symptom of many people who are clinically depressed is called self-loathing. Self-loathing is an extreme form of ownership. It can cause people to become immobilized when it comes to having the confidence to cope with everyday life. This is because this extreme form of ownership makes a person question everything he or she does. Suicide is often caused by this extreme form of self-blame. This is because the individual does not have the self-esteem and self-confidence necessary to want to live.

Yet an inability to take ownership for one's flaws, actions, or emotions can be harmful to us from a different perspective. As mentioned earlier in this chapter, over-confidence can be as detrimental as no confidence. This is because we do not take responsibility for those deficiencies or inabilities that truly get in the way of our being successful. This is sometimes referred to as "defensiveness" by psychologists. If we continually blame the external world and the people in it for our failures, we are not likely to see our contributions to our failures.

An inability to take ownership, for example, for the human tendency to be prejudiced toward people who do not hold our views makes conflict inevitable. To ignore the fact that we have personality traits that the majority of people find difficult to deal with can isolate us from social bonds that make life worth living.

A person who has exemplified this dimension is Joel Sonnenberg.

Joel Sonnenberg—Motivational Speaker

Joel Sonnenberg is probably the most unique motivational speaker of his kind. Badly disfigured in a freak car accident, Sonnenberg often tells his audiences that he is grateful to God for his disability.

When Sonnenberg was just 22 months old, a truck struck his family's car while they waited in line at a toll booth. Their car burst into flames, and Sonnenberg suffered burns over 85 percent of his body. He lost his eyelids, fingers, toes, and hair.

Sonnenberg endured incredible periods of adjustment as doctors grafted skin over his burns. For a time, he said, his home felt more like a hospital than a home, as he continued treatment.

Sonnenberg has appeared on television since age 4, inspiring others with his courage and acceptance. On his web site, he states, *"...I do consider it a privilege to look the way I do...The Lord has given me so much that I ask myself, what possibly could God give me that I haven't already received."* (*Joel Sonnenberg*, n.d.).

Initiating

> "It's all to do with the training; you can do a lot if you're properly trained."
>
> – Queen Elizabeth II

Initiating is the ability to take action on a self-problem without being forced or threatened into it by others or circumstances. Many people need external reinforcement to be motivated to change. They cannot self-motivate.

Initiating is the most critical aspect of personability because it involves action. Just because someone is *open* to new experiences, has *self-insight,* and has the ability to take *ownership* does not guarantee that he or she can act on these first three personability dimensions.

A person may be open to the possibility that he or she needs to lose weight. The person gets constant insight because he or she gets on a scale once a week and sees he or she is 50 pounds overweight. The person may take ownership that it is because of his or her eating habits and lack of exercise. Despite meeting these first three stages of personability, nothing happens.

Initiating is very difficult for several reasons. The first is often the "how" step. Having knowledge that there is a problem does not guarantee the knowledge of how to resolve it. For example, in the situation of needing to lose weight, there are a myriad of diets and exercise programs to consider. Deciding how to choose a course of action requires knowledge of each diet/exercise program's effectiveness. It also requires knowledge of a person's ability to engage in it based on his or her time, finances, and physical condition.

Once the individual has chosen a course of action to lose weight, the next step is to plan how to achieve it. It is like having a blueprint of a house being built before you build it. The financing and the time allotted must be secured before beginning. This planning ensures the likelihood of success.

The third phase of initiating is the actions that directly affect the actual outcome. This is the most difficult because it requires implementing what has been planned. This step in initiating is usually the most time consuming and requires the most self-discipline. For instance, in the example of losing weight, it might require buying certain foods, preparing certain foods, eating at a set time, and resisting the urge to go back to old eating habits. It might also require a set exercise program.

A person who has exemplified this dimension is Benjamin Carson.

Benjamin S. Carson, M.D.—Pediatric Neurosurgeon

Benjamin S. Carson, M.D., was once considered the "dummy" in elementary school, and had a temper so violent he would attack other children—and even his mother.

He eventually turned his life around, graduated from high school with honors, and went to Yale University and to medical school. At age 32, he became Director of Pediatric Neurosurgery at Johns Hopkins.

For Dr. Benjamin Carson, a well-known pediatric neurosurgeon, success did not come easily initially. His single mother raised him and his brother in inner-city Detroit, often working two or more jobs at a time to avoid having to enroll in welfare.

In fifth grade, Carson was the worst student in the class, and his peers often referred to him as "Dummy." When his mother saw his and his brother's poor grades, she immediately began limiting their TV watching and demanded that they read two library books per week and write a report on each. Even though their mother only had a third-grade education, her expectations for her sons were high.

Carson saw that he had no choice but to do what his mother asked, and as he read, he found himself acquiring knowledge, and soon, he was exceeding his teacher's and classmates' expectations, and moved to the top of the class.

(continued)

Even though Carson's academic achievement improved dramatically, Carson still faced issues with his temperament. His anger, which was constant and severe, at one point resulted in his threatening bodily harm to others. At this point, Carson made a conscious decision to pray for help in controlling his anger. He also began reading the Book of Proverbs and found that reading and praying helped him control his anger completely.

Before Carson made these changes, he was fully aware that doing poorly in school and letting his anger get the best of him would lead to failure, whether that was reform school, jail, or the grave.

By fully committing himself to self-improvement, Carson turned his life around and achieved success and fame. In addition to practicing medicine, he writes and speaks, constantly reminding his audience that there is not anything that cannot be achieved. ("Benjamin Carson Biography—Academy of Achievement," 2010).

Personality Test

Let's measure your personality potential.

Below are some questions that measure your personality skills. Answer the questions honestly. Use the following scale and place a check (✓) in the box to rate yourself for each question.

$$1 = \text{Rarely} \quad 2 = \text{Sometimes} \quad 3 = \text{Usually} \quad 4 = \text{Often} \quad 5 = \text{A Lot}$$

You may want to ask some people who know you well to rate you, using the same scale. See how closely your score and their scores match. Don't be surprised if there is a big difference.

	1	2	3	4	5
1. Do you seek criticism from significant others on how you've been acting lately?	❑	❑	❑	❑	❑
2. Do you think it's important to be self-critical?	❑	❑	❑	❑	❑

Personability Dimension

	1	2	3	4	5
3. Do you like to try different approaches to solve problems in your personal life?	❏	❏	❏	❏	❏
4. Do you like to learn about ways to improve your performances in areas of your life?	❏	❏	❏	❏	❏
5. Do you self-examine when things go wrong in your personal life? Do you consider what you might have done wrong?	❏	❏	❏	❏	❏
6. Do you try to correct mistakes you made immediately?	❏	❏	❏	❏	❏
7. Do you find it easy to admit to others when you have made a mistake?	❏	❏	❏	❏	❏
8. Could you publicly tell a large audience of people when you have made a mistake?	❏	❏	❏	❏	❏
9. Have you put in writing an apology to someone you owe one to?	❏	❏	❏	❏	❏
10. Have you always met your financial obligations to others?	❏	❏	❏	❏	❏

Scoring:

Add your total score and multiply the total by 2. This number is your ability potential in this dimension. For example: 30 × 2 = 60% ability in this range.

A score above 80% is a good score.

A score above 90% is an excellent score.

Note: A more accurate assessment of your ability in this dimension, which consists of 40 statements/questions versus the 10 shown in this book, can be found at www.sotelligence.com.

References

Alicke, M. D., & Govorun, O. (2005). The better-than-average-effect. In M. D. Alicke, D. Dunning, & J. I. Krueger (authors). *The self in social judgment: Studies in self and identity* (pp. 85 – 106). New York: Psychology Press.

Benjamin Carson Biography—Academy of Achievement. (2010, November 11). *Academy of Achievement Main Menu.* Retrieved December 16, 2010, from http://www.achievement.org/autodoc/page/car1bio-1

Carrere, S., & Gottman, J. M. (1999). Predicting divorce among newlyweds from the first three minutes of a marital conflict discussion. *Family Process, 38*(2), 293–301.

Christensen-Szalanski, J., & Bushyhead, J. (1981). Physician's use of probabilistic information in a real clinical setting. *Journal of Experimental Psychology: Human Perception and Performance, 7*(4), 928–935.

Dunning, D. (2005). *Self-insight: Roadblocks and detours on the path to knowing thyself.* New York: Psychology Press.

Dunning, D., Heath, C., & Suls, J. M. (2004). Flawed self-assessment: Implications for health, education, and the workplace. *Psychological Science in the Public Interest, 5*(3), 69–106. doi: 10.1111/j.1529-1006.2004.00018.x

Festinger, L. (1957). *A theory of cognitive dissonance.* Evanston, IL: Row, Peterson.

Gilovich, T. (1983). Biased evaluation and persistence in gambling. *Journal of Personality and Social Psychology, 44*(6), 1110–1126. doi: 10.1037/0022-3514.44.6.1110

Gladwell, M. (2008). *Outliers: The story of success.* New York: Little, Brown and Company.

Gottman, J. M., & Silver, N. (1994). *Why marriages succeed or fail and how you can make yours last.* New York: Simon & Schuster.

Herschel Walker Biography—Academy of Achievement. (2010, November 17). *Academy of Achievement Main Menu.* Retrieved December 18, 2010, from http://www.achievement.org/autodoc/page/wal0bio-1

James, W. (1890). *The principles of psychology.* New York: Dover Publications.

Joel Sonnenberg. (n.d.). Retrieved December 18, 2010, from http://www.joelsonnenberg.com/

John Wooden Biography—Academy of Achievement. (2010, June 21). *Academy of Achievement Main Menu.* Retrieved December 17, 2010, from http://www.achievement.org/autodoc/page/woo0bio-1

Loftus, E., & Wagenaar, W. (1988). Lawyers' predictions of success. *Jurimetrics Journal, 28,* 437–453.

Lord, C. G., Ross, L., & Lepper, M. R. (1979). Biased assimilation and attitude polarization: The effects of prior theories on subsequently considered evidence. *Journal of Personality and Social Psychology, 37*(11), 2098–2109. doi: 10.1037//0022-3514.37.11.2098

MacDonald, T. K., & Ross, M. (1999). Assessing the accuracy of predictions about dating relationships: How and why do lovers' predictions differ from those made by observers? *Personality and Social Psychology Bulletin, 25*(11), 1417–1429. doi: 10.1177/0146167299259007

Martin, R., & Leventhal, H. (2004). Symptom perception and health care-seeking behavior. *Psychological Science in the Public Interest, 2,* 299–328.

McRae, R. R., & John, O. P. (1992). An introduction to the five-factor model and its applications. *Journal of Personality, 60*(2), 175–215.

Pronin, E., Lin, D. Y., & Ross, L. (2002). The bias blind spot: Perceptions of bias in self versus others. *Personality and Social Psychology Bulletin, 28*(3), 369–381. doi: 10.1177/0146167202286008

Srivastava, S., John, O. P., Gosling, S. D., & Potter, J. (2003). Development of personality in early and middle adulthood: Set like plaster or persistent change? *Journal of Personality and Social Psychology, 84*(5), 1041–1053. doi: 10.1037/0022-3514.84.5.1041

Sutherland, N. S. (1994). *Irrationality: Why we don't think straight!* New Brunswick, NJ: Rutgers University Press.

Tavris, C., & Aronson, E. (2007). *Mistakes were made (but not by me): Why we justify foolish beliefs, bad decisions, and hurtful acts*. Orlando, FL: Harcourt.

Wagner, R. K. (2003). Smart people doing dumb things: The case of managerial incompetence. In R. J. Sternberg (Ed.), *Why smart people can be so stupid* (pp. 42–63). New Haven, CT: Yale University Press.

Chapter 7

Moral Dimension

> "I shall argue, no such individual would find the Golden Rule surprising in any way, because at its base lies the foundation in countless books, throughout recorded history, around the world, that is testimony to its universality."
>
> — John Locke, 1690

Morality is concerned with the goodness or badness of human behavior. It is sometimes referred to as knowing right from wrong. It is also a willingness to let accepted rules, standards, and laws determine our actions. It is most frequently associated with religion in terms of an institution that is a primary educator of moral thinking and action. Morality can also be learned through other social institutions such as family or formal education.

Words that are synonymous with morality are *ethical, good, virtuous, righteous, upright, upstanding, principled, honorable, just, decent, chaste,* and *pure.*

Most cultures have a moral code to govern the actions and thinking of its members. The most obvious example in modern Western cultures that practice Judaism and Christianity are the Ten Commandments. The Ten Commandments are universal laws of morality for those who practice the Jewish and Christian faiths.

If people were to read the *Encyclopedia of Religion and Ethics* (Hastings, Selbie, & Gray, 1980), they would soon discover that beliefs in many of the world's religions are analogous to those moral rules found in the Ten Commandments. It appears that most religions—despite their differences revolving around their politics, religious interpretations, or history—espouse the universal beliefs that oppression, murder, treachery, and falsehood are wrong and that kindness to the aged, young, and weak; charity; honesty; and impartiality are good.

A major issue regarding the powerful relationship between religion and morality is the view of many agnostics and atheists who believe, due to their questioning of God and religion, morality is not governed by religion. One of the most outspoken people is Richard Dawkins, a renowned scientist and atheist. Dawkins believes that God is a delusion and that morality has grown as a concept due to evolution. In other words, there is scientific basis for moral functioning (1997).

In the midst of these two positions is the world-renowned geneticist Francis Collins. Collins, in his book *The Language of God* (2006), takes the position that science and religion should not be opponents. Collins believes that "genetics" is God's language. Collins was an atheist until his mid-20s, and then aligned himself with Christianity. Collins takes the position that science does not know everything and that science can lead us to knowing what God is. God, according to Collins, is the genius behind our existence because our existence required a being much more superior to human capabilities.

Even Albert Einstein, a brilliant scientist and known agnostic, stated science was not substantial enough to answer all the important questions about life. Einstein said, "Science without religion is lame and religion without science is blind" (1941). Basically, the meaning of God, an afterlife, and other spiritual questions may be outside the scientific method's ability.

Within the recent decade, science has begun looking at moral functioning and spirituality from a scientific perspective. In *The Science of Good and Evil* (2004), Michael Shermer, a strong believer in Darwin and evolution, believes that moral thinking was necessary for survival reasons. Conversely, Mario Beauregard and Denyse O'Leary take the position that neuroscience can prove the existence of a soul in their book *The Spiritual Brain* (2007). They believe that the brain is God's way of leading in the right direction morally.

Regardless of the positions as to why we are moral, it is fairly clear that morality preserves our existence as a human species. The position that religion, other social institutions, and science are behind our moral thinking appears to be relevant.

Let's discuss some of the facts that relate to morality.

Fact 1: We are born to be immoral.

The belief that we are born evil has been with us since the beginning of human recorded history. It started with Adam and Eve and the taking of the forbidden fruit and original sin.

In most cultures, young children are taught to curb their natural urges from bowel control to sexual impulses. They are taught to not be violent or selfish, and they are taught to be honest and to abide by rules. It appears that our children are born to behave in immoral ways, and it is our responsibility to nurture that out of them.

The concept of sin relates to our immoral tendencies. Yet many of our immoral tendencies are necessary for our survival. Lust is defined as one of the seven deadly sins, yet lust is necessary for our survival. It is pre-programmed into our brains because Mother Nature wants us to procreate our species. Yet society does not want us to force ourselves on others sexually or to engage in nonconsensual sex. Maybe Ben Franklin had it right when he said *"Sin is not harmful because it is forbidden, but it is forbidden because it is hurtful."*

The dilemma of our inherent nature to behave in ways that are immoral but necessary to our survival creates a moral paradox. A paradox is a seemingly absurd or contradictory statement even if it is actually well-founded.

It appears our nature makes us immoral but in many ways has well-grounded reasons for it.

Fact 2: Our tendency to be moral may also be hardwired as is our tendency to be immoral.

There is a perception by some scientists that it is our nature to be moral just as it is to be immoral. In the book *Mere Christianity* by C. S. Lewis, Lewis professes a position called the "moral law of nature" (1952). According to Lewis, there is a moral code hardwired in the human species despite our culture, social sophistication, etc. Lewis professes this moral law concept in section one of *Mere Christianity*, titled "One Right and Wrong as a Clue to the Meaning of the Universe." Lewis believed that morality, despite our natural tendencies to be immoral, is also wired into our nature to increase our survival. This position again creates a moral paradox.

It could be that morality is natural to us (as well as immorality) because morality also increases our survival as a species. Human morality that professes getting along with others, being honest, trustworthy, nonviolent, etc., preserves our existence. The opposite behaviors of those above would jeopardize our survival as a species.

Antonio Damasio, a noted neuroscientist and author of the book *Descartes' Error* said:

> Looming large over the question is the issue of the origins of morality. Does reason construct moral institutions, beliefs, conventions, and rules? Or does morality emerge from prerational processes? On this issue there is growing evidence that many behaviors we designate as moral have forerunners in automated, unconscious, prerational processes, present not only in humans but in many other species. The evidence is quite robust in the case of mammals, especially primates and marine mammals whose brains share a lot with the human brain. (1994)

Damasio believes that in the case of lower mammals, morality is prewired at a less sophisticated level than humans but does exist.

In a review of the book *Wild Justice* by Marc Bekoff and Jessica Pierce, Richard Gray, a science correspondent with Telegraph.co.uk (2009), states that scientists studying animal behavior have determined that animals ranging from mice to primates are governed by moral codes of conduct in the same way as humans. Gray adds, "Until recently, humans were thought to be the only species to experience complex emotions and have a sense of morality."

In *Wild Justice,* Bekoff says that "morals are hardwired into the brains of all mammals and provide the 'social glue' that allow often aggressive and competitive animals to live together in groups" (2009). Bekoff has compiled evidence from around the world that shows that different animal species (wolves, coyotes, elephants, chimpanzees, bats, whales) have an innate sense of fairness, display empathy, and help other animals that are in distress.

And yet despite these hardwired moral codes in animals, these animals can display behavior that could be described as immoral and evil based on human terms. Jane Goodall, who studied chimpanzees as a primatologist in Gombe nearly her whole life, said, "At Gombe I thought chimps were nicer than we are. But time has revealed that they can be just as awful." She later stated that neighboring chimpanzee communities live in a permanent state of hostility and that their battles can be deadly.

It appears, then, that morality and immorality are hardwired in humans and other species in varying degrees.

Fact 3: Moral complexity is rapidly growing due to the complexity of modern society's rapid growth.

Despite its critics, Charles Darwin's theory of evolution has stood the test of time in terms of its validity. A major tenet of Darwin's theory is that species have to adapt to their environment to survive and those that do not adapt will not survive. These adaptive changes are so slow that our sense of them is not obvious.

In their recently published book, *The 10,000 Year Explosion,* Cochran and Harpending discuss civilization accelerating human evolution. They argue that our biology explains the expansion of the Indo Europeans, the European conquest of the Americas, and the European Jews' rise to intellectual prominence. They claim the key to these advancements was recent genetic change due to evolution adaptation (Cochran & Harpending, 2009). For example, milk tolerance in early Indo European civilizations allowed for a new way of life from being hunter-gatherers to domesticating for food animals.

The authors' discussions range from subjects such as human domestication to skin pigmentation changes to eye color changes to increasing IQ test scores. These rapid changes convincingly demonstrate the power of human genetics and adaptation (Cochran & Harpending, 2009).

If our civilization is growing rapidly in terms of complexity such as our ancestors' use of the quill tip pen to write 200 years ago to a laptop computer today, a moral adaptation has to take place simultaneously.

The proliferation of laws reflects society's growing need to address the constantly changing world of what is right and wrong. This rapid change is reflected in many cross-cultural disagreements of what is morally right. The stoning of a woman for adultery in one culture is acceptable and morally right but is abhorrent in another culture. A father's right to kill his daughter for shaming his family is acceptable in some cultures but not in others.

The landscape of what is criminal is also changing. The term *cybercrime* did not exist 25 years ago. The development of computers has provided society with a rapid flow of information but brought with it new methods of being immoral. The fact that someone can hack into a computer system and do harm to a multitude of people with the push of a button has changed our moral landscape. Our modern world has brought advances in quality of life but also advances in how to be immoral.

Fact 4: What is moral and immoral depends on what we are taught rather than our inherent nature.

Context refers to the circumstances in a given situation. The same action may therefore be considered moral in one context and not in another. The most extreme example is the act of killing someone. The "Thou shalt not kill" commandment is a general statement that implies killing someone is always immoral regardless of the context.

Yet the context of killing may influence the degree of immorality. For example, planning and committing a murder of someone who has offended you is not the same as killing someone while driving drunk nor is it the same as killing someone while driving sober. Yet does the difference between murder, negligent manslaughter, and non-negligent manslaughter determine the consequences and the moral culpability one receives for killing someone?

In *On Killing,* Dave Grossman takes the position that killing is not natural for most of us. In other words, the majority of us humans have to be taught to kill. Grossman, a retired Lieutenant Colonel Army Ranger, says that following World War II, the U.S. government instituted a program to increase the kill rates of soldiers in combat (Grossman, 2009).

During World War II, U.S. Army Brigadier S.L.A. Marshall undertook a survey of thousands of American troops directly after combat. He found that only 20 percent of soldiers actually shot at the enemy even when under attack. Marshall concluded that it was a fear of killing, not the fear of being killed, that caused battle failure. At the most critical point of battle, Marshall states soldiers became conscientious objectors. It appears that most soldiers by nature believe that killing is immoral. Grossman says that the kill rate in the Vietnam War was 100 percent due to a change in military training since World War II. Soldiers were taught that killing was not immoral in the context of war.

Fact 5: The ability to have feelings is critical to our ability to be moral.

In Jonah Lehrer's *How We Decide,* he suggests that reasoning is insufficient in deciding what is moral. He uses psychopaths as an example. Psychopaths initially appear to be perfectly rational people. They also possess great working memories, excellent language skills, and good attention spans. Several studies show psychopaths have above average IQ (Lehrer, 2009).

Based on the above, one would assume that an intelligent person knows right from wrong. Yet psychopaths are more likely to use violence to achieve their goals. According to Lehrer, psychopaths are over-represented in our prisons. Lehrer believes that the problem with psychopaths is caused by damaged emotional parts of their brain, which implies that a lack of emotion causes psychopaths to be immoral.

Damasio, cited earlier, says that certain social emotions such as compassion, admiration, shame, guilt, gratitude, and pride embody moral values. These social emotions act as moral regulators for how we treat others in our everyday lives. Guilt and shame, for example, which psychopaths do not seem to possess, help us regulate our behavior by self-punishing ourselves when we do something wrong or immoral. As described by Damasio, these social emotions are sometimes referred to as moral emotions (1994).

Conversely, emotions have often been associated with immoral acts. For example *anger* can cause us to harm someone. *Fear* can cause us to act cowardly in the face of adversity. *Laziness* can cause us to be irresponsible. *Envy* can cause us to be socially harmful. And *lust* can cause us to be socially irresponsible.

It may be that emotions, as they relate to moral functioning, need to mature just as reasoning does. It also appears that emotion and reasoning must work together rather than act as separate entities to achieve moral competence. For example, it may be that I see a homeless person and choose to give him or her money because I feel compassion for that person and reason that I am more fortunate and should give something back to society in general. Conversely, a family member/friend has committed a serious crime we have knowledge of. We decide we have to come forward with this information despite our caring about the friend or relative, because we reason it is morally the right thing to do.

In both of the above instances, feelings and reasons were considered in deciding a course of action even though the feelings and reasons may be in conflict with each other.

Fact 6: Laws are necessary to ensure moral behavior.

Laws, rules, and policies are critical to ensuring moral conduct. Human nature tends to be self-serving. It is wired into us genetically according to Richard Dawkins in his well-publicized book, *The Selfish Gene*. Dawkins proposes that all species are genetically wired for self-preservation, and he brings forth a significant amount of science to support his position (2006).

A considerable amount of immoral behavior is caused by our self-serving tendencies. Cheating on a test, stealing money or property, not telling the truth if it makes us look bad, taking credit when things go right and blaming when they do not, imposing our will and beliefs on others to validate our own, and even gossiping that could denigrate the image of another are caused by this self-serving tendency. Dawkins would say these self-serving tendencies are necessary to any species' survival (2006).

To control these self-serving tendencies, laws are developed. Probably the main objective of laws is to ensure what might be called *fairness to all*. The Ten Commandments are Jewish and Christian general laws that ensure fairness. The United States Constitution ensures the fairness of the U.S. government and fair treatment of its citizens.

A major aspect of the law is not only the laws themselves, but those who enforce and interpret the laws' applications. One of the most simplistic examples of the need for laws is the need for rules in sports. For example, in the game of baseball, the umpire is both the enforcer and interpreter of rules. The umpire's job is to ensure fairness whereas the players would most likely choose fairness that meets Dawkins's self-serving tendencies of all species.

The umpire behind home plate determines whether a pitcher has thrown a ball or strike. The first base, second base, and third base umpires maintain fairness in the field of play by determining if someone is safe or out. If these details were left up to the players, fairness based on facts versus personal perceptions would be in great jeopardy.

Ensuring the laws on a baseball field is much easier than doing so in greater society because the actions of the players are managed by the umpire moment to moment. Every action exhibited by a player is under the watchful eye of the umpire. Also the action of the players is measurable or can be quantified in tangible terms. This makes it easier to interpret evidence of moral behavior.

In the greater society, the application of laws is much more difficult to account for than in sports. People are not under the constant watchful eye of an umpire. Most of the general laws of society are very broad when it comes to determining someone's guilt or innocence versus someone being out or safe. This lack of constant monitoring by a neutral eye coupled with an inability to measure moral behaviors in simple terms, as in baseball, can cause a higher degree of immorality to occur. It is obvious we need laws, rules, etc., but it is not a failsafe system in terms of accuracy.

Fact 7: Sometimes being legal can be immoral.

Laws are created to define what immoral behavior is and to punish those who choose to violate them. Without laws (in other words, lawlessness), the chances of immoral actions go up significantly.

In October 2010, the United States Supreme Court had to decide a case involving free speech. The case involves Matthew Snyder, a Lance Corporal killed in Iraq, versus Fred Phelps and members of the Westboro Baptist Church.

Fred Phelps and members of his congregation demonstrated at Snyder's funeral with signs that read *"Thank God for Dead Soldiers," "Fag Soldiers,"* and *"Pope in Hell."* The members of this church also posted on the Web a video about their protests. The video indicated that Snyder's father and mother taught Matthew to defy his Creator and raised him for the Devil.

Snyder's father sued Westboro Baptist Church for damages. Initially, Matthew Snyder's father won his lawsuit against the Westboro church. His case was reversed in the United States Supreme Court of Appeals. The court said "as utterly distasteful as these Westboro Baptist Church signs are they involve matters of public concern and hence are protected under the free speech law provided by our Constitution."

It is obvious to most of us that picketing at funerals, especially at those of fallen soldiers, is immoral. It shows a lack of respect for the deceased and of regard for the pain and suffering of the bereaved. Despite this behavior, it may not be illegal despite being, as one jurist put it, "utterly distasteful."

In the above instance, the United States Supreme Court had a major dilemma. The jurists had to ignore their innate sense of morality to ensure the right to free speech.

Oftentimes, law enforcement officers find themselves in situations where enforcing the law creates a moral dilemma. This is referred to as officer discretion. An officer might make an arrest but does not agree with the law supporting it. On the opposite side, officers know they may have a guilty party in a crime, but due to the legal process, the offender escapes just consequences. This legal/moral dilemma is one of the major stressors for law enforcement officers.

Fact 8: Morality is a constantly evolving phenomenon that is affected by societal changes.

In October 2010, a Rutgers University student was videotaped by a college roommate having a homosexual encounter. The student having the homosexual encounter was unaware he was being videotaped by his roommate. The roommate later placed the video on a Website where others were able to view it. Mortified, the videotaped student ultimately committed suicide. The question in this scenario is whether the roommate videotaping the homosexual encounter is morally culpable and possibly legally responsible for his actions.

In the past several years, DNA testing has been used to determine criminal guilt or innocence, and many prisoners have been released who were initially convicted of serious crimes. Conversely DNA is also increasing the probability of connecting criminals to past crimes that may not have been possible before.

Current social media technologies such as Facebook, Twitter, and blogs are constantly changing the moral nature of our world. Cybercrime is defined as any illegal act that involves a computer. Since the term has come about, several sub-types of cybercrime have been given their own names. Such sub-types include hacking, virus generation, theft of communications, cyberstalking, cyberbullying, and transmission of pornographic material involving children. Recently added to the list of cybercrimes is illegal gambling on the Internet.

It is obvious the more complex our world becomes, the broader are our possibilities of immorality and how they are defined. Some actions show up on our internal radars as immoral, but no laws have been established that define them as illegal. It often takes time for laws to catch up with certain immoral behaviors.

Some people respond to society's inability to keep up with immoral but not illegal behavior with the Golden Rule. The Golden Rule refers to the philosophy of "treat others only as you consent to being treated in the same situation." It requires that we be consistent in behaving or acting toward others in ways that are in harmony with our own desires.

Donald Pfaff's *The Neuroscience of Fair Play: Why We (Usually) Follow the Golden Rule* argues that the Golden Rule is hardwired in, just as Dawkins argues that we are innately selfish (Pfaff, 2007; Dawkins, 1997). Pfaff would say that environment and learning can influence our morality, but most of us know right from wrong in our guts even if we do not have a law/rule against it. We are wired for good behavior as well as bad behavior. We therefore should know the good or moral thing to do when there are no rules. It comes down to asking oneself how he or she would feel if it were being done to him or her. It appears some people do not understand appropriate behavior unless there are rules, however.

Fact 9: Morality needs to be studied as a science and not just a philosophy.

Morality has been studied as a philosophy. According to *The New Oxford American Dictionary*, a philosophy is the use of reason or logic in seeking truth and knowledge of reality, especially the causes and natures of things. The mission of philosophy is to try to understand principles that govern reality.

Morality has rarely been studied as a science. A science is defined as the systematic observation of and experiment with phenomena to try to determine the principles that govern reality.

Both philosophy and science seek truth. Of the two, science is seen as significantly more reliable in determining truth. There are several reasons for this. The first reason is that science removes as much of the human bias as possible. Philosophy does not, because it relies permanently on a human reasoning that cannot remove human bias.

Another reason science is more reliable is that it requires systematic research, which removes not only human bias, but also what is called *error variance*. Error variance occurs when factors that occur in nature cause false conclusions about the truth. Eye witness testimony has a lot of error variance, which makes it unreliable, but DNA has very little error variance. Therefore, DNA is much better at determining truth than eye witness testimony because DNA has significantly better controls for error variance.

The third reason science is more reliable is because it requires replication to increase its ability to seek truth. Replication involves repeating the research experiments several times and seeing if the results are always the same. An example would be measuring the effectiveness of a drug by running several experiments. If repeated experiments are used and the results are the same, the drug's effectiveness is seen as more reliable. If the repeated experiments of the drug give mixed results, then its effectiveness is less reliable. Reliability refers to consistency, and consistency increases truth.

In studying morality as a science and not as philosophy, truth increases. The simplest example of this is the debate in sports regarding instant replay in determining the accuracy of an umpire's judgment in baseball. An umpire is supposed to be objective, and that should remove human error. Umpires try, but their humanity can get in the way. A camera is not human and looks at truth—i.e., safe or out, strike or ball—in a scientific way. When the camera keeps looking at a play from several angles, it is trying to remove error variance and increase the truth.

In applying the scientific approach to legalizing and not legalizing marijuana, the intent would be determining the objective cost versus benefits for one or the other. For example, if the scientific method was used to decide, rather than the philosophical view, the discussion to continue laws against it or not would be more accurate. This type of study would be an immense undertaking but more accurate than the philosophical debate.

Consider this: Philosophy did not create airplanes and allow humans to fly. Science did. Philosophy did not create the cure for polio. Science did.

Fact 10: The Golden Rule may transcend culture, nations, and countries and may be universal in most humans.

The Golden Rule, as described earlier, is hardwired in us to preserve our existence. Jordan Grafman, who is Chief of the Cognitive Neuroscience at the National Institute of Neurological Disorders and Stroke, found that virtue (the Golden Rule) literally has its own reward in how it affects the brain (McGowan, 2009).

Neuroimaging shows that the brain's altruistic behavior (giving rather than getting) sends reward-related brain systems into a pleasurable tizzy—even more than self-interest gain. According to Grafman, "The big punchline is that all things being equal, your reward system fires off a lot more when you're giving than when you're taking. It appears that good is better than being evil as far as the brain is concerned" (McGowan, 2009).

It may be that pride, envy, greed, wrath, lust, gluttony, and sloth—the Seven Deadly Sins—may be rewarding, but they are not as rewarding as restraint from committing them. So when we experience a spark of lust, greed, or wrath, or sudden desire to hit somebody there may be a struggle in our brains where the sinful reward system and virtual reward system battle it out.

It may be that we are wired to sin, but excessive indulgence in wrath, lust, and/or greed eventually catches up with and in fact predicts our doom.

Developing and Applying Your Moral Ability

Accountable Ability

> "Honesty is the first chapter of the book of wisdom."
>
> – Thomas Jefferson

Accountability is the ability to be liable, responsible, or answerable. It requires people to realize that their actions have to be taken into account. They cannot avoid their responsibility in any situation.

An accountant keeps records of his or her clients' finances so that they do not misuse their money. Legal counsel makes us accountable for keeping our actions within the law. Parents teach their children that they have to be accountable for their education so that they know how to have a better life.

Moral accountability refers to one's ability to know right from wrong. Many religions use the cliché that we will be held accountable when we meet our maker. When someone admits they made a mistake such as stealing something or telling a lie, they are making themselves accountable. In Catholicism, the act of confessing sins to a priest makes Catholics accountable to God, which results in reconciliation. Reconciliation means to make one friendly again after estrangement.

In a work environment, accountability could also mean evidence that is documentable. This overlaps into Fact 9 above, where science tries to be more accountable for truth than philosophy does.

An example of this issue was the initial decision to enter into our current war with Iraq. A main reason for invasion was the belief that Iraq possessed weapons of mass destruction (WMD). Opponents to the invasion believed there was not enough proof that Iraq possessed such weapons. The proponents of the war argued there was, so the invasion proceeded. It became apparent that WMD were not present as first believed, but the war continued.

Secretary of Defense Colin Powell was initially a proponent of the invasion but came to realize WMD were not present. He was the first to admit that he was wrong to have taken the position that there were WMD. Despite Powell's admission, most of President Bush's administration believed that

Powell was wrong. It appears that Powell's position to be accountable for being wrong did not sit well with the rest of the administration. Powell eventually resigned only to be vindicated later.

The issue in the above incident is that moral accountability is easier to achieve when the level of truth supports the assertion being made. Powell was also respected by most of the public despite the disfavor he had with the administration ("Colin Powell Biography—Academy of Achievement," 2010).

A person who has exemplified this dimension is Ralph Nader.

Ralph Nader—Consumer Crusader

Ralph Nader was the epitome of citizen accountability. In his book, *Unsafe at Any Speed*, Nader took on the American automobile industry in terms of safety accountability for the cars they produce.

Nader has devoted his life to accountability. From a very young age, when he was a student at Princeton, Nader found problems and sought solutions to them. A regular hitch-hiker, Nader realized in his travels that there seemed to be too many fatal automobile accidents. He deduced that while driver error often caused accidents, unsafe vehicles had much to do with whether the accidents were fatal.

Nader eventually wrote a best-selling book, *Unsafe at Any Speed*, which led to the automobile industry changing its standards. Of course, the automobile industry was reluctant to admit any fault or make changes, and openly criticized Nader. At one point, General Motors even hired private detectives to try to derail Nader's efforts. Nader would not be silent. *"A good citizen is not just a person who votes all the time,"* Nader said ("Ralph Nader Biography—Academy of Achievement," 2011).

Over the years, Nader took other important consumer issues on his shoulders, including pollution and access to information. Always the consummate advocate for corporate and government accountability, Nader was instrumental in creating the Environmental Protection Agency and the Freedom of Information Act.

Principled Ability

> "Rules of society are nothing; one's conscience is the umpire."
>
> – Madame Dudevent

A principle is defined as a fundamental truth or law that is determined by reason or action. A fundamental truth of science is H_2O always equals water. A fundamental law in social relationships is that human actions determine human reactions. In other words, how I treat others determines how I am treated.

There are many principles in life that do not guarantee a 100 percent outcome as in the water example above. Human actions determining human reactions falls in the uncertain outcome category. This type of scientific principle only implies high probability of an outcome and not a guaranteed one. For example, you may be friendly toward a person (an action) and assume he or she will be friendly in return (reaction). There is high probability he or she will (based on social science research regarding social mimicry), but there is no guarantee.

A principled person therefore acts on the premise that following a certain set of principles in daily life will consistently produce certain outcomes. He or she tries not to stray from that principled path despite the temptation to do so.

Individuals may decide that being honest in keeping their word is a principle they have to live by every day. But they may run into a situation like owing someone money, and circumstances prevent them from paying the loan back on time. There is no written record of the loan. They now have three options: (1) they can avoid the person they owe money to by not returning calls; (2) they can deny the loan was ever made (no written record); or (3) they can call the person and tell them they cannot pay the loan at this moment but intend to by a certain date. They can commit to paying added interest on the loan or provide collateral to insure the loan will be paid.

Obviously the third option is the principled option. Despite circumstances that prevented the loan being paid by a particular time, steps were taken that displayed two moral competencies. The person was accountable by taking responsibility and was principled by keeping a promise despite there being no written record of the debt.

An actual example of being principled despite pressure not to be was Senator Oscar Underwood of Alabama, a former presidential candidate (1912) and a former Democratic floor leader in both the House and Senate who was urged that he say nothing that could offend the Ku Klux Klan, then a rising power particularly in Southern politics. But Senator Underwood, who was convinced that the Klan was contrary to all the principles of Jeffersonian democracy in which he believed, denounced the Klan in no uncertain terms. He attempted to establish an anti-Klan plank in the party platform. As a result, the Louisiana delegation and other Southern political groups publicly repudiated him, and his chances for being nominated for the presidency were quashed. Further, Underwood also was never re-elected to Senate in his home state of Alabama. Senator Underwood's principles drove his actions despite the fact that it was unpopular to do so.

A person who has exemplified this dimension is Frank M. Johnson, Jr.

Frank M. Johnson, Jr.—Federal Judge

Frank M. Johnson, Jr., shaped the civil rights movement. In the state of Alabama, African-Americans could count on impartial justice in Judge Johnson's courtroom. He never backed down even when his mother's home was bombed by the Ku Klux Klan.

Johnson was not a typical white Southerner. He did not align himself with Southern Democratic ideologies (he joined the Republican Party), and he did not subscribe to the belief that African-Americans were not equal to whites.

(continued)

The Supreme Court dismissed the "separate but equal" doctrine in 1954, and after President Eisenhower appointed Johnson as judge of the U.S. District Court in middle Alabama, his principles were put to the test almost immediately. As the South tried to come to terms with the new law, and some jurists dragged their feet, Johnson applied the new standard in decision after decision, beginning with a case involving the segregation of Montgomery's bus system.

The public and even former friends ostracized Johnson for his decisions. He and his family were constantly threatened—students burned a cross in his yard, and his mother's house was bombed.

Despite the pressure and isolation, Johnson never wavered. *"I wasn't hired to be a moral judge or a preacher or an evangelist. I'm hired to apply the law,"* he said ("Frank Johnson Biography—Academy of Achievement," 2006).

Courageous Ability

> "Courage is not simply one of the virtues, but the form of every virtue at the testing point."
>
> – C. S. Lewis

Courage is defined by *The New Oxford American Dictionary* as an ability to disregard fear. It is also defined as the ability to face extreme dangers and difficulty without retreating and further defined as the ability to endure times of adversity. Words that are synonymous with courage are *guts, resolute, tenacious, nerve, boldness, gallant,* and *brave.*

Moral courage is an ability to maintain a moral action despite adversity to do so. It could involve the maintenance of rule despite its unpopularity. It could involve going against a rule that could be immoral if employed.

Let's take the example of imposing a law or rule despite its unpopularity. You are a coach of a university football team. Your star quarterback has recently been arrested and convicted of a DUI. The rule is a player who is arrested and convicted for DUI is automatically suspended for three games. You know that you will be facing the best team you will play all season the second game of your quarterback's suspension. You choose to impose the suspension despite the pressure from all sides. You impose the rule to communicate to all players that the rules apply to everyone despite the consequences.

Choosing not to impose a law or rule because to do so would be immoral can be problematic. Such a choice could legally jeopardize the person not enforcing the law. This is a dilemma that many police officers face every day. Pretend you are a police officer. You pull over a vehicle for speeding (30 miles over the speed limit). As you approach the vehicle, the male driver gets out of the car. He appears to be very emotional, so much so that you believe some misfortune has befallen him. When you ask him for proof of insurance, etc., and he starts to mumble, "I can't have one more thing go wrong," you decide to let him talk. He tells you that he has just lost his job. As you talk with him further, you find out he has three small children and his wife works part time. You decide to give him a warning because the ticket would be $300, plus it would affect his car insurance premium.

Someone who willingly endures negative perception, words, actions, and emotions could be labeled as someone who is trying to act morally. The best example of this type of courage is President Gerald Ford who pardoned President Richard Nixon from involvement in the Watergate scandal. Nixon resigned as president of the United States in 1972. Gerald Ford was the vice president at that time and assumed the role of president. Many Americans wanted Nixon to suffer the full consequences of his actions. Yet Ford realized that America needed to heal from the wounds of Watergate, and he was the only one who could do it. He pardoned Nixon one month after becoming president, knowing that it would cost him the presidency. Later, Ford was accused of letting Nixon off because Ford was Nixon's vice president. Ultimately, Ford lost his bid for president by a narrow margin to Jimmy Carter in 1976.

A person who has exemplified this dimension is Rosa Parks.

Rosa Parks—Pioneer of Civil Rights

In December of 1955, Mrs. Rosa Parks was a seamstress in Montgomery, Alabama, when she refused to give up her seat on a city bus to a white passenger. The bus driver had her arrested. She was tried and convicted.

When Rosa Parks refused to give her bus seat to a white person on December 1, 1955, she had no idea of the fire it would spark. Her innocuous refusal led to her arrest, and once word spread, African-American anger bubbled over.

With the help of Dr. Martin Luther King, Jr., who was just the pastor of Dexter Avenue Church in Montgomery, a boycott of the bus system began. A domino effect ensued, and most agree that the Civil Rights Movement was born of Parks's simple act of courage.

"I don't remember feeling that anger, but I did feel determined to take this as an opportunity to let it be known that I did not want to be treated in that manner and that people have endured it far too long. However, I did not have at the moment of my arrest any idea of how the people would react," Parks said in an interview about her refusal to stand up ("Rosa Parks Interview—Academy of Achievement," 2010).

Altruistic Ability

> "Even if it's a little thing, do something for those who have need of help, something for which you get no pay but the privilege of doing it."
>
> — Albert Schweitzer

Altruism is defined as having regard for others as a principle for action. People who are altruistic are seen as unselfish, giving, caring, humane, charitable, public spirited, empathic, and self-sacrificing.

Altruistic ability is listed as the fourth dimension under moral ability because it is probably the core factor that drives moral actions. Most immoral behavior involves actions toward others not toward oneself. If altruism drives my thinking, feelings, and actions, then I would always take into consideration how my actions affect others.

A decision to not steal something from someone may be deferred for three reasons, for example. The first reason is "I don't want to get caught and suffer public scorn." A possible second reason may be my religious belief of "Thou shalt not steal" because my God may punish me. The third reason to not steal is how I would feel if someone stole from me. This third reason is driven by altruism; I defer to how you would feel. I may selfishly want to have the item I am stealing, but my selflessness says it would hurt the person from whom I am stealing it.

Altruism is the core morality motivator because our motives are internalized. They are a part of us. When morality is motivated by external threats such as legal consequences, public scorn, or fear of being sinful, it is not as pure.

Selfishness is the core factor in moral behavior because you come first. Dawkins, mentioned earlier, believes that we are genetically wired to preserve ourselves over others (Dawkins, 2006). This self-preservation instinct is in all living things and is necessary to reproduce and ensure the survival of our offspring. It is about competition for survival.

The counter to Dawkins's view is that altruism is the cornerstone to our survival. Without altruism, our species would not survive. Rudolph Rummel indirectly addresses the issue of altruism versus selfism in his book *Power Kills: Democracy as a Method of Nonviolence*. Rummel concluded after studying over 371 wars (since the early 1800s) that there has never been a war between two democratic societies. There have been wars between democratic and nondemocratic societies and wars between nondemocratic societies. Democratic societies stress the rights and needs of everyone. The United States Constitution advocates religious freedom, and the ideals that all men are born equal and have the right to free speech, etc. These tenets are altruistic philosophies (Rummel, 1997).

There is a third position that advocates a middle ground between altruism and selfism—utilitarian values must be considered when deciding what is moral. This position supports the belief that an immoral act must be considered because a greater moral outcome can occur. It argues that altruism is fine for many situations but could, on the other hand, allow immorality to continue.

An example of this is the decision that was made to drop the atomic bomb on Japan in World War II. It was speculated that a land invasion would result in a significant number of American soldiers being killed or wounded. The dropping of the bomb would not.

In this scenario, the immoral act of dropping the atomic bomb on Hiroshima and Nagasaki was moral because it would end the war without the significant loss of American lives. It was also reasoned that the Japanese surprise attack on Pearl Harbor was a highly immoral act, so American retaliation was just. What made the use of the bomb moral was the utilitarian view of moral. An altruist would have never sanctioned the use of the atomic bomb.

It could be that altruism could have prevented our war with the Japanese. If the Japanese leadership was altruistic prior to World War II, the war would have never occurred.

A person who has exemplified this dimension is Paul Farmer.

Paul Farmer, M.D.—Founder, Partners in Health

For nearly 30 years, Paul Farmer, M.D., has brought first rate medical care to the poorest people on earth. He built a first rate hospital in Haiti. In his book, *Pathologies of Power*, he denounces the structural violence that denies millions of people the most basic human rights, i.e., allowing the destitute to be attended to.

For 30 years, Farmer has worked tirelessly to bring better medical treatment to the disadvantaged. Collectively, he spent much of his time in poverty-ravaged Haiti, working to control infectious diseases there.

Such community-based infectious disease control in the poorest countries is the focus of Farmer's work. Farmer also founded Partners in Health (PIH), an organization whose mission is not only to provide medical care but to promote its moral duty to serve the disadvantaged. Sometimes this comes in the form of pressuring and lobbying those with the means to support the PIH mission.

"For me, an area of moral clarity is: you're in front of someone who's suffering and you have the tools at your disposal to alleviate that suffering or even eradicate it, and you act," Farmer said ("Paul Farmer Biography—Academy of Achievement," 2010).

Morality Test

Let's measure your morality potential.

Below are some actions that measure your morality skills. Rate the statements honestly. Use the following scale and place a check (✓) in the box to rate yourself for each statement.

1 = Rarely   2 = Sometimes   3 = Usually   4 = Often   5 = A Lot

You may want to ask some people who know you well to rate you, using the same scale. See how closely your score and their scores match. Don't be surprised if there is a big difference.

	1	2	3	4	5
1. When I make a decision, I take into account how that decision could affect other people.	❏	❏	❏	❏	❏
2. I confront people who put me in situations that go against my sense of right and wrong.	❏	❏	❏	❏	❏
3. I think there can be a difference between legal action and ethical action.	❏	❏	❏	❏	❏
4. I would be willing to question a rule or policy that doesn't make sense before applying it.	❏	❏	❏	❏	❏
5. I would take into account how I am feeling before I apply a rule or policy that affects another person.	❏	❏	❏	❏	❏
6. I believe that honesty and truth are not the same thing.	❏	❏	❏	❏	❏
7. I think moral decision making should take into account how one's emotions affect that decision.	❏	❏	❏	❏	❏
8. I would feel uneasy if I had to enforce a rule or policy that hurts someone.	❏	❏	❏	❏	❏

	1	2	3	4	5
9. I believe that the enforcement of some laws by the legal system can cause an immoral action to occur.	❏	❏	❏	❏	❏
10. I think that a lot of decisions have to be made that affect people negatively.	❏	❏	❏	❏	❏

Scoring:

Add your total score and multiply the total by 2. This number is your ability potential in this dimension. For example: 30 × 2 = 60% ability in this range.

A score above 80% is a good score.

A score above 90% is an excellent score.

Note: A more accurate assessment of your ability in this dimension, which consists of 40 statements/questions versus the 10 shown in this book, can be found at www.sotclligence.com.

References

Beauregard, M., & O'Leary, D. (2007). *The spiritual brain: A neuroscientist's case for the existence of the soul.* New York: HarperOne.

Bekoff, M., & Pierce, J. (2009). *Wild justice: The moral lives of animals.* Chicago: University of Chicago Press.

Cochran, G., & Harpending, H. (2009). *The 10,000 year explosion: How civilization accelerated human evolution.* New York: Basic Books.

Colin Powell Biography—Academy of Achievement. (2010, November 11). *Academy of Achievement Main Menu.* Retrieved December 18, 2010, from http://www.achievement.org/autodoc/page/pow0bio-1

Collins, F. S. (2006). *The language of God: A scientist presents evidence for belief.* New York: Free Press.

Damasio, A. R. (1994). *Descartes' error: Emotion, reason, and the human brain.* New York: Putnam.

Dawkins, R. (1997). Is science a religion? *The Humanist, 57,* 26–29.

Dawkins, R. (2006). *The selfish gene.* Oxford: Oxford University Press.

Einstein, A. (1941). *Science and religion.* Address presented at Conference on Science, Philosophy, and Religion in Their Relation to the Democratic Way of Life, Inc. New York.

Frank Johnson Biography—Academy of Achievement. (2006, March 26). *Academy of Achievement Main Menu.* Retrieved December 17, 2010, from http://www.achievement.org/autodoc/page/joh2bio-1

Gray, R. (2009, May 23). Animals can tell right from wrong. *The Telegraph,* n. p.

Grossman, D. (2009). *On killing: The psychological cost of learning to kill in war and society.* New York: Little, Brown and Company.

Hastings, J., Selbie, J. A., & Gray, L. H. (1980). *Encyclopedia of religion and ethics*. Edinburgh: T. & T. Clark.

Lehrer, J. (2009). *How we decide*. Boston: Houghton Mifflin Harcourt.

Lewis, C. S. (1952). *Mere Christianity*. New York: Macmillan.

Marshall, S. L. (2000). *Men against fire: the problem of battle command*. Normal, OK: University of Oklahoma Press.

McGowan, K. (2009, September). I didn't sin—it was my brain. *Discover Magazine*. doi: http://discovermagazine.com/2009/sep/05-i-didn.t-sin-it-was-my-brain

Paul Farmer Biography—Academy of Achievement. (2010, May 12). *Academy of Achievement Main Menu*. Retrieved December 18, 2010, from http://www.achievement.org/autodoc/page/far1bio-1

Pfaff, D. W. (2007). *The neuroscience of fair play: Why we (usually) follow the Golden Rule*. New York. Dana Press.

Ralph Nader Biography—Academy of Achievement. (2011, January 12). *Academy of Achievement Main Menu*. Retrieved December 18, 2010, from http://www.achievement.org/autodoc/page/nad0bio-1

Rosa Parks Interview—Academy of Achievement. (2010, September 20). *Academy of Achievement Main Menu*. Retrieved December 16, 2010, from http://www.achievement.org/autodoc/page/par0int-1

Rummel, R. J. (1997). *Power kills: Democracy as a method of nonviolence*. New Brunswick (U.S.A.): Transaction.

Shermer, M. (2004). *The science of good and evil: Why people cheat, gossip, care, share, and follow the Golden Rule*. New York: Times Books.

The New Oxford American Dictionary. (2005). New York: Oxford University Press.

About the Author

Sotelligence

The Pioneer In Social Intelligence Skills

Steve J. Sampson, Ph.D.
Founder, President

Dr. Steve Sampson has been teaching social intelligence, conflict resolution and interpersonal skills for over 30 years. He brings both academic knowledge and practical experience to his seminars.

As an Educator, he holds a Bachelors Degree in Sociology from the University of Massachusetts (1970) and a Masters (1976) and Doctoral Degree (1981) in Counseling Psychology from Georgia State University. He is a nationally recognized Master Trainer in Interpersonal Communication Skills since 1977, and has presented that training to over 300 agencies and organizations in 40 states. He is a former Assistant Professor of Criminal Justice at Georgia State University from 1979 to 1985. More recently, he retired from his position as a Clinical Professor in the Counseling and Psychological Services department at Georgia State University (1995–2004). He is currently an Executive-in-Residence Professor at the College of Justice and Safety at Eastern Kentucky University (2009–present).

As a Licensed Psychologist, he is the former Chief of Psychology of Georgia Regional Hospital, Atlanta, Georgia (1993–1995). He is also a nationally recognized counseling psychologist who works with various law enforcement agencies conducting fitness for duty evaluations and post shooting debriefings since 1982. He has been a contract Psychologist with 25 Metropolitan Atlanta Law Enforcement Agencies since 1991. Dr. Sampson has been conducting management training since 2003 for several federal government agencies (FBI, NSA, DEA, USSS, and DOE).

As a Criminologist, Dr. Sampson is the former correctional superintendent for Massachusetts Halfway Houses Inc. (1969–1973), as well as the
former Correctional Superintendent for the Georgia Department of Correc-
tions (1974–1976). He has provided training to over 250 prisons, law
enforcement, and public safety agencies in Social Skills Training since 1977.

As an author, he has published the following books on Social Intelligence
Skills:

Social Intelligence Skills for Government Managers
Social Intelligence Skills for Law Enforcement Supervisors/Managers
Social Intelligence Skills for Correctional Supervisors/Managers
How to be in a Personal Relationship
Applied Social Intelligence
Leaders without Titles